D1121359

PROBLEM SOLVING
Step-By-Step

Metropolitan Teaching and Learning Company
33 Irving Place
New York, New York 10003

Printed in the United States of America

ISBN: 1-58120-705-0

10 9 8 7 6 5 4 3 2

STEP 5 • Table of Contents

STEP 5 • Topics

Tables

1.3 Reading Tables
5.1 Using a Table to Rename Measures
9.2 Making a Rate Table

Bar Graphs

1.2 Reading Bar Graphs
4.6 Reading a Double-Bar Graph

Line Graphs

4.2 Reading a Line Graph
4.3 Interpreting Changes in a Line Graph

Circle Graphs

4.5 Reading a Circle Graph

Multi-Step Problems

2.4 Writing a Word Equation
3.5 Solving Multi-Step Problems
10.2 Deciding How to Estimate
10.3 Writing a Word Equation
10.4 Writing Word Equations

Estimation/Number Sense

1.1 Eliminating Wrong Answer Choices
2.1 Estimate or Exact Answer?
2.2 What Is the Question?
6.1 Using Benchmarks
7.2 Is the Computed Number the Answer?
10.4 Writing Word Equations

Representing Problems Differently

3.1 Using Simpler Numbers
3.6 Writing an Equivalent Problem
5.2 Deciding How to Rename Customary Measures
5.3 Deciding How to Show Measures Another Way
7.1 Drawing a Picture to Rename Measures
7.3 Using Models
10.3 Writing a Word Equation

Proportional Thinking

9.1 Writing Equal Ratios
9.2 Making a Rate Table
9.3 What Are the Units?

Algebraic Thinking

2.4 Writing a Word Equation
7.1 Drawing a Picture to Rename Measures
8.1 Explaining the Problem in Your Own Words
8.2 Drawing a Number Line
10.3 Writing a Word Equation
11.1 Using Formulas

Visual Thinking

4.1 Organizing a List
7.3 Using Models
10.1 Drawing a Number-Line Segment
11.2 Drawing Examples
12.1 Making a Table to Show Possible Outcomes
12.2 Making a Tree Diagram

Answer Interpretation

2.1 Estimate or Exact Answer?
2.2 What Is the Question?
3.3 Interpreting the Quotient
3.4 Which Answer Makes Sense?
7.2 Is the Computed Number the Answer?
9.3 What Are the Units?

Recognizing Important Information

2.3 Underlining Information
3.2 Underlining Information
4.4 Finding Data in a News Article
6.2 Drawing a Number Line

Eliminating Wrong Answer Choices

Deciding what to do first can help you solve a test problem more easily. One way to begin is to eliminate answer choices that are clearly wrong.

Example

A. Read the problem carefully. Then look at the information given in the table. The table shows the longest and shortest distances from Earth of several planets. What is the shortest distance between any of these planets and Earth?

Distances to Planets in Our Solar System		
Planet	Shortest Distance from Earth	Longest Distance from Earth
Mars	35,000,000 mi	248,000,000 mi
Venus	25,000,000 mi	161,000,000 mi
Saturn	745,000,000 mi	1,031,000,000 mi

A 35,000,000 mi
B 1,031,000,000 mi
C 25,000,000 mi
D 10,000 mi

B. Look at each answer choice. Compare the answer choices with the distances given in the table.

- Choice B appears in the table under the "Longest Distance" category, so this choice cannot be correct. Cross out choice B.

- Choice D does not appear in the table, so it cannot be correct. Cross out choice D.

- The two remaining choices are A and C. Both choices appear in the table under the heading "Shortest Distance." Circle these choices.

C. To solve the problem, you need to compare only two choices instead of four.

Compare: 25,000,000 < 35,000,000

So, the correct choice is _____ miles.

GUIDED PRACTICE

Use the table to answer the questions.

Distances to Planets in Our Solar System		
Planet	Shortest Distance from Earth	Longest Distance from Earth
Mars	35,000,000 mi	248,000,000 mi
Venus	25,000,000 mi	161,000,000 mi
Saturn	745,000,000 mi	1,031,000,000 mi

1. Which choice shows the planets in order from farthest to nearest when each planet is at its farthest from Earth?
   A Mars, Saturn, Venus
   B Mars, Venus, Pluto
   C Saturn, Mars, Venus
   D Venus, Mars, Saturn

   a. Which answer choice contains a planet that is not in the table? _____ Cross out this answer choice.

   b. Which answer choice shows the planets in order from nearest to farthest?

      _____ Cross out this answer choice.

   c. Compare the remaining choices: A and C. Which choice shows the

      planets in order from farthest to nearest? _____

2. The greatest distance from Earth to the sun during Earth's revolution around the sun is 94.6 million miles. Which choice below shows this number in standard form?
   J 94 million, 6 hundred thousand
   K 94,600,000
   L 90,000,000 + 4,000,000 + 600,000
   M 9,460,000,000

   Cross out each answer choice that you find to be wrong.

   a. Which answer choices are not written in standard form? _____

   b. Answers K and M are not crossed out. Is there a fast way to eliminate one of them? Explain.

   _____

   c. The correct answer to the problem is _____.

6

Name _____

PRACTICE

Use the table below to answer problems 3–8. You may want to cross out answer choices that are clearly wrong to help you solve each problem.

Magnitudes of Some Stars

Star	Magnitude
Vega	0.04
Rigel	0.14
Procyon	0.37
Betelgeuse	0.41
Achernar	0.51

> The brightness of a star is called its magnitude. The lower the magnitude, the brighter the star.

3. What is the magnitude of the brightest star named in the table?

   A 0.51
   B 0.37
   C 0.16
   D 0.04

4. What is the magnitude of the least-bright star named in the table?

   J 0.03
   K 0.51
   L 0.41
   M 0.14

5. What is the difference in magnitude between Rigel and Procyon?

   A 0.0023
   B 0.023
   C 0.23
   D 2.3

6. What is the difference in magnitude between Procyon and Betelgeuse?

   J 0.004
   K 0.04
   L 0.4
   M 4.0

7. What is the difference in magnitude between the brightest and the least-bright star?

   A 0.02
   B 0.47
   C 2.06
   D 2.47

8. What is the name of the brightest star in the table?

   J Capella
   K Achernar
   L Vega
   M Rigel

● Comparing and Ordering

Use the table below to solve problems 1–5. Fill in the box of your choice in the space at the bottom. You may want to cross out clearly wrong choices.

Distance of Planets from Sun

Planet	Distance from Sun
Earth	93,000,000 mi
Jupiter	484,000,000 mi
Mars	142,000,000 mi
Mercury	36,000,000 mi
Neptune	2,800,000,000 mi
Pluto	3,700,000,000 mi
Saturn	888,000,000 mi
Uranus	1,800,000,000 mi
Venus	67,000,000 mi

1. Based on the information in the table above, which planet do you think has the closest average distance from Earth?
   A Mars
   B Neptune
   C Pluto
   D Venus

2. About how many times as far from the sun is Pluto than Mercury?
   J about 36 times as far
   K about 10 times as far
   L about 1,000,000 times as far
   M about 100 times as far

3. Which answer choice shows the distances of the four closest planets to the sun in order from greatest to least?
   A 36,000,000; 67,000,000; 93,000,000; 142,000,000
   B 484,000,000; 900,000,000; 2,800,000,000; 3,700,000,000
   C 142,000,000; 93,000,000; 67,000,000; 36,000,000
   D 142,000,000; 67,000,000; 93,000,000; 36,000,000

4. Which planet is the middle planet?
   J Earth
   K Saturn
   L Jupiter
   M Not given

Write About It

5. Look again at problem 3 above. Explain how you solved the problem.

   _____

   _____

   _____

   _____

   _____

1. A ☐ B ☐ C ☐ D ☐   3. A ☐ B ☐ C ☐ D ☐

2. J ☐ K ☐ L ☐ M ☐   4. J ☐ K ☐ L ☐ M ☐

● Comparing and Ordering

Reading Bar Graphs

To solve a problem, you sometimes have to find the
information you need by reading a bar graph. Begin by looking
at what the different parts of the graph tell you.

The graph at the right shows the
maximum speeds of four mammals. The
vertical axis is labeled **Speed** and shows
the speeds in kilometers per hour. The
horizontal axis is labeled **Mammal**. It
shows the name of the mammal for each
data entry.

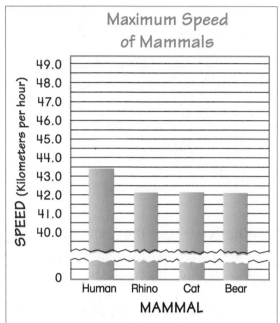

The speeds in this graph are not exact.
They have been rounded.

Example 1

What is the maximum speed of a human?

> **Step 1:** Look for the bar that is
> labeled Human. The length of the bar
> shows you a human's maximum speed.
>
> **Step 2:** Find the top of the bar. Move across the
> graph to the vertical axis.

When a graph has a
break, like this one, it
means that all of the
data is greater than the
top edge of the break.

**The top of the bar is halfway between what two
numbers?**

_____ and _____

So, the maximum speed of a human is

_____ **kilometers per hour.**

Notice the two
intervals between
43.0 and 44.0.
The line in between
shows 43.5.

Example 2

Which mammal has a maximum speed of
45.0 kilometers per hour?

> **Step 1:** Find the bar that stops at 45.0 kilometers per hour.
>
> **Step 2:** Follow the bar to the horizontal axis.

Which name is below that bar? _____

So, the _____ has a maximum speed of 45.0 kilometers per hour.

● Comparing and Ordering Numbers   9

Bar graphs can also be horizontal. Use the graph below to answer the questions.

1. What year had the fastest winning time?
   Step 1: Look at the table. Find the shortest bar.
   Step 2: Look across the bar.

   What year is the bar for? _____

   So, _____ was the year with the fastest winning time.

2. At a track meet, the winning time for the women's 200-meter run is 0.4 second slower than the winning Olympic time in 1988.
   What is the winning time at the track meet?

   Step 1: Find the bar for 1988. **Where does the bar stop?** _____ seconds
   Step 2: Add.

   0.4 + _____ = _____ seconds

   So, the winning time at the track meet is _____ seconds.

3. **What is the combined time of all the winning times?**
   Step 1: Find the time that each bar shows.

   1980 _____ s   1988 _____ s   1996 _____ s

   1984 _____ s   1992 _____ s

   Step 2: **Add the times for each year.**

   _____ + _____ + _____ + _____ + _____ = _____ s

   So, the combined time for all the years is _____ seconds.

Read the bar graph to find the information you need. You may mark or draw on the graph.

4. **What is the distance that Barry ran?** _____ **kilometers**

5. **Put the runners in order from the runner who ran the greatest distance to the runner who ran the least.**

   _____

6. **What does the break in the graph mean?**

   _____

   _____

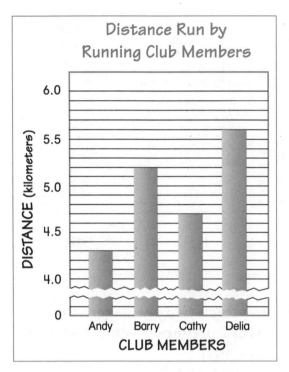

7. Tulin ran 1.3 kilometers farther than Delia ran.

   How far did Tulin run?

   _____

8. Cathy is training for a race. The race is 5 kilometers long. Before she runs in the race, she wants to be training at that distance.

   How much farther does Cathy need to run in order to train at the distance of the race?

   _____

9. The coach of the track club wants to know the total distance run by the four runners in the graph.

   What is the total distance that the four runners ran?

   _____

10. Last week Andy ran 2.2 kilometers less than the distance shown in the graph.

    How far did Andy run last week?

    _____

TEST-TAKING PRACTICE

Use the bar graph to solve the problems. Choose the best answer for each problem.

1. In which two years were the winning times greater than 37.5 seconds?
   A 1980 and 1984
   B 1980 and 1992
   C 1984 and 1992
   D 1992 and 1994

2. At a regional meet, the winning time in the 500-meter event is 1.3 seconds slower than the time in 1988.

   What is the winning time at the regional meet?
   J 35.3 seconds
   K 37.9 seconds
   L 71.3 seconds
   M 71.6 seconds

3. What does the break in the graph mean?
   A In every year, the winning skaters finished in under 36.0 seconds.
   B In every year, the winning skaters finished in over 36.0 seconds.
   C The skaters who did not win all finished in under 36.0 seconds.
   D Not given

Write About It

Write a plan for solving the problem, and then solve it.

4. What is the total combined time of all the winners from 1980 to 1994?

   _____

   _____

   _____

   _____

   _____

   _____

1. A ☐ B ☐ C ☐ D ☐

2. J ☐ K ☐ L ☐ M ☐

3. A ☐ B ☐ C ☐ D ☐

● Comparing and Ordering Numbers

Reading Tables

Sometimes, the information you need to solve a problem is in a table.

A. The title and labels of a table tell you what the table is about. **What is the table at the right about?**

_____

_____

B. The **data**, or pieces of information, in a table are given in columns and rows. The first column in this table is labeled "Region." **What data are in the "Region" column?**

_____

_____

What data are in the "Area" column?

_____

_____

Land Area of World Regions

Region	Area (in millions of square miles)
Africa	11.7
North America	9.4
South America	6.9
Antarctica	5.4
Asia	17.4
Europe	3.8
Oceania (including Australia, New Zealand)	3.3

C. What is the land area of Africa?

Step 1: Find "Africa" in the first column.
Step 2: **Draw a line to the number *in the same row* of the second column.**
This number shows the land area of Africa in millions of square miles.

So, the land area of Africa is _____ million square miles.

D. Which region has the greatest land area?

Step 1: Compare the numbers in the second column. Find the greatest number.
Step 2: **Draw a line to the name of the region in the same row.**
This is the region with the greatest land area.

So, the region with the greatest land area is _____.

GUIDED PRACTICE

Complete the table, and answer the questions.

Gold Person Triathlon Results

Athlete	Swim	Bicycle	Run	Total Time
Frank	25 min	46 min	55 min	_____ min
Janice	_____ min	53 min	52 min	_____ min
Leore	23 min	_____ min	67 min	_____ min

1. What is this table about?

   _____

   _____

   _____

2. Janice had the fastest time in the Swim. She finished in 21 minutes. **In the table, fill in Janice's swim time.**

   Step 1: Find Janice's name in the table.

   Step 2: Move your finger across the row to the **Swim** column. Fill in her time.

3. Who had the fastest time in the Run?

   Step 1: Find the **Run** column in the table.

   Step 2: Move your finger down the **Run** column, and find the shortest time.

   Step 3: Move your finger along the row with the shortest time to the name column.

   So, _____ had the fastest time in the Run.

4. Leore finished the Bicycle part of the race in 35 minutes.

   In the table, fill in her time.

Solve . . . .

Use the information in the table to solve each problem.

5. **Who had the fastest time in the Bicycle part of the race?**

   _____

6. **Who had the slowest time in the Swim?**

   _____

7. **What was Leore's time in the Run?**

   _____ minutes

8. **Who had the fastest time in all three parts of the race combined? In the Total Time column fill in the total times for each person.**

   So, _____ had the fastest total time.

14

PRACTICE

Use the table to find the information you need to solve the problems. You may mark or draw lines on the table.

World Areas and Populations by Region

Region	Area (square miles)	Population 1994
North America	9,400,000	289,000,000
South America, Caribbean	6,900,000	474,000,000
Europe	3,900,000	509,000,000
Asia	17,200,000	3,344,000,000
Africa	11,700,000	701,000,000
Oceania (including Australia, New Zealand)	3,300,000	28,000,000
Antarctica	5,100,000	0

9. What is the table about?

_____

_____

10. What data does the third column give you?

_____

_____

11. What is the area of Oceania?

_____

12. What was the population of Oceania in 1994?

_____

13. Which region has an area of 5.1 million square miles?

_____

14. Which region had a population of 509,000,000 in 1994?

_____

15. Which region had the largest population in 1994?

_____

16. Which region had the smallest population in 1994?

_____

TEST-TAKING PRACTICE

Use the table to solve the problems. Choose the best answer for each problem. In the answer section at the bottom of this page, fill in the box of your choice.

Populations of Four of the World's Largest Cities

City	Population (millions in 1998)	Population (estimated millions in 2015)	Annual Growth Rate (percent)
Bombay	15.1	26.2	4.2
Mexico City	16.5	19.2	1.8
New York City	16.3	17.6	0.3
Tokyo	27.0	28.9	1.5

1. **In the first two columns, what do the numbers show?**

   A number of cities in the world
   B number of people in a city
   C number of people in the world
   D number of people in a country

2. **Which of the following sentences is false?**

   J In the table, Tokyo is a city.
   K The table has a column called "Annual Growth Rate."
   L The table has a row called "New York City."
   M Tokyo's population in 1998 was 26 million people.

3. **Which city has an Annual Growth Rate of 0.3 percent?**

   A Bombay   C New York City
   B Mexico City D Tokyo

Write About It

Write a plan for solving the problem, and then solve.

4. **Which city has the least difference between its population in 1998 and its estimated population in 2015? How many more people will it have?**

   _____

   _____

   _____

   _____

   _____

   _____

1. A ☐ B ☐ C ☐ D ☐   3. A ☐ B ☐ C ☐ D ☐

2. J ☐ K ☐ L ☐ M ☐

© 1999 Metropolitan Teaching & Learning Co.

16

• Numeration and Comparing

Estimate or Exact Answer?

Deciding on the kind of answer you need can often help you to solve a problem. Sometimes, you can estimate. At other times, you need an exact answer.

Example 1

Tony has $5. He wants to buy pretzels and a 2-liter bottle of soda for a party. Does he have enough money?

Because the problem does not ask for a price or for a money amount, you do not need an exact answer. You can estimate to find out whether Tony has enough money.

Snack Price List	
Pretzels	$1.89
Crackers	$1.99
Nuts	$2.19
2-liter soda	$1.59

Step 1: Estimate how much the two items will cost.

THINK: Round each number to the next-higher dollar.

$1.89   + $1.59
  ↓   ↓

$2   + $_____   = $_____

So, the two items cost about $ _____.

Step 2: Because you rounded up, your estimate is higher than the exact sum would be. Compare the money Tony has to the estimated cost of the two items.

$5 > $4

Does Tony have enough money to buy both items? _____

Example 2

Janice has $11. Does she have enough money to buy one package of nuts each week for 4 weeks?

Step 1: Round the cost of a package of nuts to the nearest dollar.

Round $2.19 to $_____.

Step 2: Multiply to find the total cost of 4 packages of nuts.

4   x $_____   = $_____

$_____ < $11

Does Janice have enough money? _____

● Multiplication and Division

1. Alex had $10. He bought 20 stamps for $6 at the post office.
   How much money does he have left?

   Does the problem require an exact answer, or can you estimate? Explain.

   _____

   Solve the problem. $_____ − $6 = $_____

   So, Alex has $_____ left after buying 20 stamps.

2. Is the sum of 33, 87, and
   48 greater than 200?
   **Does the problem require an
   exact answer, or can you
   estimate? Explain, then solve.**

   _____

   _____

   _____

   Step 1: Round each number up.

   Round 33 up to _____.

   Round 87 up to _____.

   Round 48 up to _____.

   Step 2: **Add.**

   _____

   Step 3: **Compare the sum to 200.**

   _____

   Is the sum of 33, 87, and 48 greater

   than 200? _____

3. In 1998, the Science Museum had
   155,398 visitors. In 1999, it had
   182,045 visitors. About how many
   more people visited the museum
   in 1999 than in 1998?

   **Does the problem require an
   exact answer, or can you
   estimate? Explain.**

   _____

   _____

   Solve.

   Step 1: Round both numbers to
   the nearest ten thousand.
   Round 155,398 to 160,000.

   Round 182,045 to _____.

   Step 2: **Subtract.**

   _____ − _____ = _____

   **The museum had about _____
   more visitors in 1999 than in 1998.**

PRACTICE

Decide whether you must give an exact answer or an estimate. Then solve.

4. Jennifer earns $9 per week. She wants to buy her mother a clock that costs $50. If she saves for 4 weeks, will she have enough money?

_____

_____

Will Jennifer have enough money?

_____

5. An amusement park had 342,981 guests in June and 478,982 guests in July. About how many people visited the parks in the two months?

_____

_____

About _____ people visited the park in June and July.

6. Ed has $175 to spend on tires for his van. If each tire costs $37, how many tires can he buy?

_____

_____

Ed can buy _____ tires.

7. Tyrone works at a computer store. A customer buys $238 worth of software. He gives Tyrone $300. How much change should the customer receive?

_____

_____

The customer should receive $_____ in change.

8. A CD player at Flower Records costs $149. The same CD player at Bob's Dust Jacket costs $125. About how much more does the CD player cost at Flower Records?

_____

_____

The CD player costs about $ _____ more at Flower Records.

9. Tayonna bought a jacket for $24 and a shirt for $11. How much did she spend?

_____

_____

Tayonna spent $ _____.

Choose the best answer for each problem. In the answer section at the bottom of this page, fill in the box of your choice.

1. The stadium at the Ashland School seats 375 people. **If every game is sold out, about how many games will it take to sell 1,600 tickets?**

   A 1 game   C 3 games
   B 2 games   D 4 games

2. Sylvia is making three shelves for her kitchen. One shelf is 16 inches long, another is 17 inches long, and the third is 18 inches long. If she cuts the 3 shelves from one board, what is the shortest length the board can be?

   What kind of answer do you need?

   J an estimate
   K an exact answer
   L a money amount
   M a rounded-up number

3. Jackie bought a box of cards for $4.00. She gave the cashier a $10 bill. **How much change should she receive?**

   A $4.00   C $6.00
   B $5.00   D $7.00

4. Mel makes $19 a week mowing lawns. **About how long will it take him to save $100?**

   J 1 week   L 4 weeks
   K 2 weeks   M 5 weeks

5. The art museum had 819 visitors today. **If each visitor paid $6, about how much money did the museum take in?**

   A $400   C $4,800
   B $800   D $5,400

Write About It

For this problem, decide whether you need an exact answer or an estimate. Then write a plan for solving the problem, and solve it.

6. **Charles wants to buy a pair of shoes for $50. He has $29 now. How much more money does he need to buy the shoes?**

   _____

   _____

   _____

1. A ☐ B ☐ C ☐ D ☐   4. J ☐ K ☐ L ☐ M ☐
2. J ☐ K ☐ L ☐ M ☐   5. A ☐ B ☐ C ☐ D ☐
3. A ☐ B ☐ C ☐ D ☐

● Multiplication and Division

What Is the Question?

Some math problems that involve numbers ask for an answer that is not a number. Explaining a problem in your own words can help you identify the question you are being asked. It can also help you decide on the kind of answer you need.

Example 1

Jeremy grows fruit. He makes fresh-fruit baskets and sells them. For each basket, he needs 45 minutes to pick the fruit, clean it, and arrange it in the basket. A customer calls to order 7 baskets. The customer says she needs the baskets in 4 hours. Does Jeremy have enough time to fill the order?

A. Rewrite the question in your own words.

Is the time it takes Jeremy to make 7 baskets greater than or less than 4 hours? If it is greater, he cannot fill the order. If it is less, he can.

B. How much time does it take Jeremy to make 7 baskets?

$45 \times 7 = 305$ minutes

C. Solve the problem that you wrote.

4 hours = 240 minutes

305 > 240

No, Jeremy does not have enough time to fill the order.

Example 2

Jeremy grows fruit. He makes fresh fruit-baskets and sells them. For each basket, he needs 45 minutes to pick the fruit, clean it, and arrange it in the basket. How long does it take Jeremy to make 2 baskets?

A. Is the answer to this question a number? _____

When a question asks for a number, you usually do not need to rewrite it.

B. Solve the problem.

$2 \times 45 =$ _____ minutes

So, it takes Jeremy _____ to make 2 baskets.

1. Derrick is helping to raise money to build a new concert hall in his town. The Arts Committee has offered an award to anyone who raises $2,000. Derrick raised the following amounts over 4 weeks: $348, $750, $406, $813. Did Derrick raise enough money to earn an award?

   a. Is the answer to this question a number? _____

   b. Rewrite the question in your own words.

      If the sum of the amounts that Derrick raised over 4 weeks is greater than or equal to $ _____, he receives an award.

   c. Solve your problem.

      $348 + 750 +$ _____ $+$ _____ $=$ _____

   Is the sum greater than or equal to $2,000? _____
   Answer the question.

   _____

2. How much more would Derrick have to raise to earn a second award?

   a. Is the answer to this question a number? _____

   Even though this problem asks for an exact answer, you may still find it helpful to rewrite the question in your own words.

   b. Rewrite the question in your own words.

   How much more is the amount needed for 2 awards than the amount of money Derrick raised in 4 weeks?

   c. Solve your problem.

      _____ $- 2,317 =$ _____

   Answer the question.

   _____

PRACTICE

For problems 3 and 4, rewrite the question in your own words. Then solve.

3. Sam leaves work at 5:30 P.M. It takes him 1 hour and 15 minutes to edit 1 page. If it is 1:45 P.M., will he have time to edit 3 pages before he leaves?

_____

_____

_____

_____

Will Sam have enough time to edit 3 pages before he leaves work?

_____

4. Adam plays harmonicas. He has harmonicas in 5 keys. If each harmonica cost $19.95, how much did it cost him to buy all 5?

_____

_____

_____

_____

It cost Adam $ _____ to buy 5 harmonicas.

Solve . . . .

5. A large office is moving. Each of the 80 people who work in the office has 2 boxes.

    a. If the truck moving the boxes can take 30 boxes in one trip, will the boxes all be moved in 5 trips?

    _____

    b. If it costs the company $15 to move each box, how much does the move cost in all?

    _____

6. Liz and Ben are making a quilt. They need at least 5 yards of fabric. The fabric costs $25.67 a yard. Ben has $59, and Liz has $87.

    a. Do they have enough money to buy the fabric they need?

    _____

    b. How much more money would Liz and Ben need to buy fabric for another quilt?

    _____

Choose the best answer for each problem. In the answer section at the bottom of this page, fill in the box of your choice.

1. Saul sells books. Each book costs him $4.95. He resells each book for $7.00. A customer wants to buy 150 books in bulk for a total of $742.50. Does Saul still make a profit?

   Which sentence is a way to rewrite the problem?

   A The difference between $4.95 and $742.50 is the profit Saul makes.

   B If 150 times $4.95 is less than $742.50, Saul makes a profit.

   C If $742.50 divided by 150 is less than or equal to $4.95, Saul makes a profit.

   D The profit is $7.00 multiplied by 150.

2. A tall building has 14 steps from each floor to the next. **If Jannette walks 169 steps from the bottom floor will she make it to the 14th floor?**

   J yes L 12.071
   K no M 155

3. Eduardo has averaged 1.92 goals per game over the last 3 seasons he has played soccer. **Going by his average, about how many goals should he score in 16 games?**

   A about 16 C about 36
   B about 32 D about 48

Write About It

Rewrite the problem in your own words. Then solve.

4. **Mario makes patterns with tiles. In one pattern, he uses 5 orange squares, 3 white diamonds, and 4 green triangles. He has all the orange squares and white diamonds he needs. If Mario repeats the pattern 345 times, will 1,450 green triangles be enough?**

   _____

   _____

   _____

   _____

   _____

1. A ☐ B ☐ C ☐ D ☐   3. A ☐ B ☐ C ☐ D ☐
2. J ☐ K ☐ L ☐ M ☐

● Multiplication

Name _____

Chapter 2 L3

Underlining Information

Sometimes, a problem contains more information than you need. You can underline information in the problem to help you focus on the information you need to solve it.

Example

Camille takes people on walking tours. She visits interesting sites in the city where she lives. She takes a maximum of 8 people on each tour. The cost of the tour is $3.75 per person. Each tour takes 90 minutes. The tour goes to 6 places. The last stop on the tour is a chocolate factory. On Monday, 29 people sign up for tours. How many tours will Camille need to lead to provide a tour for everyone who signed up?

A. Read the problem carefully. Think about the question the problem asks. The question you need to answer is the last sentence:

> **How many tours will Camille need to lead to provide a tour for everyone who signed up?**

Ring the question in the problem.

B. Now go back to the problem. What information do you need to answer the question?

> **She takes a maximum of 8 people on each tour.**
> **On Monday, 29 people sign up for tours.**

Underline the information that you need in the problem.

C. To find the number of tours, divide the number of people by the number on each tour.

$$29 \div 8 \rightarrow \underline{\hspace{2cm}}$$

The quotient means there are 3 groups of 8 people with 5 people left over.

So, to take all 29 people on tours, Camille must lead _____ tours.

GUIDED PRACTICE

Use the problems below to answer questions 1 and 2. They have the same information as the problem on page 25, but you need to underline different information to find the answers.

Version A

Camille takes people on walking tours. She visits interesting sites in the city where she lives. She takes a maximum of 8 people on each tour. The cost of the tour is $3.75 per person. <u>Each tour takes 90 minutes. The tour goes to 6 places.</u> The last stop on the tour is a chocolate factory. On Monday, 29 people sign up for tours.

Version B

Camille takes people on walking tours. She visits interesting sites in the city where she lives. <u>She takes a maximum of 8 people on each tour. The cost of the tour is $3.75 per person.</u> Each tour takes 90 minutes. The tour goes to 6 places. The last stop on the tour is a chocolate factory. On Monday, 29 people sign up for tours.

1. How much does Camille earn for one tour if the maximum number of people sign up for it?

   a. **Which version has the information underlined that you need to solve this problem?**

   _____

   b. **Solve the problem.**

   8 x _____ = $ _____

   So, Camille earns $ _____ on one tour if the maximum number of people sign up for it.

2. If the tour has 12 minutes walking time, how much time can be spent at each stop on the tour?

   a. **Which version has the information underlined that you need to solve this problem?**

   _____

   b. **Solve the problem.**

   _____ − _____ = _____ minutes

   _____ ÷ _____ = _____ minutes

   So, _____ minutes can be spent at each stop.

PRACTICE

Problems 3—6 use the same information. For each problem, ring the question you need to answer and underline the information you need to answer it.

3. Tim is reading a book about ancient Egypt. The book is 375 pages long. The book contains many photos of Egyptian art and architecture. Tim estimates that he reads 15 pages each night before he goes to bed. Someday he hopes to visit Egypt. He begins reading at 9:00 o'clock each evening.

   If he continues to read the book at the same rate, how many days will it take him to read the whole book?

   _____

4. Tim is reading a book about ancient Egypt. The book is 375 pages long. The book contains many photos of Egyptian art and architecture. Tim estimates that he reads 15 pages each night before he goes to bed. Someday he hopes to visit Egypt. He begins reading at 9:00 o'clock each evening.

   If it takes Tim 5 minutes to read each page, at what time does he finish reading?

   _____

5. Tim is reading a book about ancient Egypt. The book is 375 pages long. The book contains many photos of Egyptian art and architecture. Tim estimates that he reads 15 pages each night before he goes to bed. Someday he hopes to visit Egypt. He begins reading at 9:00 o'clock each evening.

   If a round-trip ticket to Egypt costs 3 times the number of pages in the book, how much does a round-trip ticket cost?

   $_____

6. Tim is reading a book about ancient Egypt. The book is 375 pages long. The book contains many photos of Egyptian art and architecture. Tim estimates that he reads 15 pages each night before he goes to bed. Someday he hopes to visit Egypt. He begins reading at 9:00 o'clock each evening.

   If Tim finished reading tonight at 10:30, how long did it take him to read each page?

   _____ minutes

Use the information below to answer problems 1–3. Choose the best answer for each problem.

Jenna runs a business making deliveries by truck. One day she picks up a load of 120 crates of oranges to deliver to 3 different locations. She collects $5.35 for each crate that she delivers to a customer. The first delivery is to a grocery store. Jenna and her assistant take 23 minutes to unload 42 crates. The next delivery is to a fruit stand, and it takes 25 minutes. All but 30 crates are delivered. The final delivery takes 14 minutes.

1. How many crates are left after the second delivery is made?

    What information do you not need to answer the question?
    A   One day she picks up a load of 120 crates.
    B   The first delivery is to a grocery store. She and her assistant take 23 minutes to unload 42 crates.
    C   She collects $5.35 per crate that she delivers.
    D   The next delivery is to a fruit stand and it takes 25 minutes. All but 30 crates are delivered.

2. **How much time in all did Jenna and her assistant spend unloading crates?**
    J   48 min   L   14 min
    K   62 min   M   1 h

3. **What is the total amount of money Jenna collected from the second delivery?**
    A $103.45   C $256.80
    B $220.10   D   Not given

Write About It

In the problem at the top of the page, underline the information you need to answer this question. Write a plan for solving the problem, and then solve.

4. **How much longer did the first delivery take than the final delivery?**

    _____

    _____

    _____

    _____

    _____

1. A ☐ B ☐ C ☐ D ☐   3. A ☐ B ☐ C ☐ D ☐
2. J ☐ K ☐ L ☐ M ☐

Name _____

Writing a Word Equation

When solving a multi-step word problem, you may find it helpful to explain the problem in your own words and write a word equation.

Example

Hattie and Murphy have collected 14 pounds of aluminum cans for a hospital fund-raiser. Each pound is worth $1.25. They want to raise a total of $20. How much more money do they need to raise?

A. Write a word equation to describe the problem.

Total money – Money collected = Money needed
   ↓   ↓   ↓
  $20   **?**   **?**

B. You know the total ($20), but you don't know how much money Hattie and Murphy have already collected. Write a word equation to describe *just that part* of the question.

Pounds of cans x **Dollars per pound** = **Money collected**
   ↓   ↓   ↓

_____ x _____ = $_____

C. You know the *pounds of cans* and the *money per pound* so you can solve the first equation.

Total Money – **Money collected** = **Money needed**
   ↓   ↓   ↓

_____ – _____ = $_____

D. Answer the question:

Hattie and Murphy need to raise $ _____ more.

© 1999 Metropolitan Teaching & Learning Co.

GUIDED PRACTICE

1. Josiah and Gabriel have collected 45 pounds of cardboard for a town fund-raiser. Each pound is worth $0.25. They want to raise $15. How much more money do they need to raise?

   a. Write a word equation to describe the problem.

   Total money – _____ = **Money needed**

   b. Write a word equation describing the money already collected, and then solve it.

   Pounds of cardboard x Dollars per pound = Money collected

   _____ x **$0.25** = _____

   c. You know the total money and the money collected, so you can solve the first equation and answer the question.

   _____ – _____ = **Money needed**

   _____ – _____ = _____

   So, Josiah and Gabriel need to raise $ _____ more dollars.

2. Josiah takes 10 pounds of cardboard to a recycling company that pays $0.25 per pound. Gabriel takes 15 pounds to another company that pays $0.40 a pound. How much more money than Josiah does Gabriel earn?

   a. Write a word equation to describe the problem.

   _____ – **Money Josiah earns = More money
   Gabriel earns**

   b. Solve.

   So, Gabriel earns $ _____ more than Josiah.

Name _____

PRACTICE

The table below shows the amounts of different items found in a 100 pound sample of garbage. Use the table to answer the questions.

Different Items Found in Garbage (100 total pounds)

Item	Amount in pounds
paper products	38
food wastes	7
yard wastes	18
metals	8
glass	7
plastics	8
rubber, leather, textile, and wood	14

source: U.S. Environmental Protection Agency

3. How much heavier are the paper products than the combined weight of food and yard wastes? **Write word equations, and then solve.**

_____

_____

_____

_____

The weight of paper products is _____ pounds greater than the combined weight of food and yard wastes.

Solve . . . .

4. **How much heavier is the combined weight of rubber, leather, textile, wood, and plastics than the combined weight of metals and glass?**

_____

_____

_____

5. Suppose you doubled the amount of garbage in the sample by looking at a 200-pound sample of garbage. **How many pounds heavier would the metals be than the glass?**

_____

_____

_____

Use the table to solve the problems. Choose the best answer for
each problem.

Recycling Collections in Duncan

Recycling Item	Week 1	Week 2	Week 3
cans	345 lb	295 lb	298 lb
newspapers	576 lb	682 lb	598 lb
glass	259 lb	332 lb	416 lb
plastics	132 lb	137 lb	281 lb

1. For Week 1, the amount of
nonrecyclable garbage was half
the weight of the cans and
newspapers combined. How
heavy was the nonrecyclable
garbage?

   **Which equation could not be
   used to solve the problem?**

   A weight of cans + weight
   newspapers = weight of cans
   and newspapers combined.
   B weight of cans and
   newspapers combined ÷ 2 =
   weight of nonrecyclable
   garbage.
   C 345 + 576 = 921 pounds
   D 345 ÷ 2 = weight of
   nonrecyclable garbage.

2. How much more plastic was
collected during Week 3 than the
combined total amount collected
in Week 1 and Week 2?
   J 5 lb   **L** 149 lb
   K 12 lb   **M** 269 lb

3. **How many more pounds of
recyclables were collected in
Week 2 than in Week 1?**
   A 110 lb   **C** 134 lb
   B 132 lb   **D** 137 lb

Write About It

Write word equations for solving the
problem, and then solve.

4. **How much more newspaper was
collected in Week 2 than the total
amount of plastics collected in all
three weeks combined?**

   _____

   _____

   _____

   _____

   _____

   _____

   _____

1. A ☐ B ☐ C ☐ D ☐   3. A ☐ B ☐ C ☐ D ☐

2. J ☐ K ☐ L ☐ M ☐

● Multiplication and Division

Test-Taking Skill: Writing a Plan

Some questions on tests ask you to explain how you solve a problem. Write a plan to show the steps you take. Show your calculations.

Example 1

How many more people lived in Midland City in 1860 than in 1835?

Population of Midland City

Year	Population
1853	207,089
1860	813,669
1995	7,322,564

A. **Read the problem carefully. Decide on the kind of answer you need.**

The answer called for is the difference between a city's population in 1860 and in 1835.

B. **Write a plan for finding the answer.** First, I will look in the second column of the table to find the population figures. Then, I will subtract to find the difference.

C. **Follow your plan, and answer the question.**

Population in 1860 – Population in 1835 = Difference in population

813,669   – 207,089   = _____

A total of _____ more people lived in

Midland City in 1860 than in 1835.

Example 2

Was the population growth in Midland City greater between 1835 and 1860 or between 1860 and 1995?

A. **Decide on the kind of answer you need, and write a plan.**
I need to find the time interval in which the difference in population was greater. I already found the difference for the time interval between 1835 and 1860 in **Example 1.** I will have to find the difference for the time interval between 1860 and 1995 and then compare the two differences.

B. **Follow the plan, and answer the question.**

Population difference from 1835 to 1860: _____

Population difference from 1860 to 1995: 7,322,564 – 813,669 = _____

_____ > _____

So, the population growth from 1860 to 1995 was _____ than the

population growth between 1835 and 1860.

Public Libraries Systems		
City	Population Served	Number of Books
Los Angeles, California	3,681,708	5,743,103
San Antonio, Texas	1,310,500	1,754,291
Toronto, Ontario	637,049	2,087,863
Detroit, Michigan	1,027,974	2,804,428

Use the table. Write a plan to solve each problem. Follow your plan, and solve.

1. How many people does the library with the fewest books serve? Which city is it in?

_____

_____

_____

_____

_____

_____

_____

_____

2. How many more people are served by the library system that serves the largest population than the one that serves the smallest population? Name the systems.

_____

_____

_____

_____

_____

_____

_____

_____

_____

_____

● Test-Taking Skill

Using Simpler Numbers

Sometimes, using simpler numbers can help you to solve a problem.

The table below shows the numbers of calories used during different exercises by a person who weighs 100 pounds.

Calories Used During Exercises

Activity	Calories Used Per Minute
walking	2.7
jogging	6.1
volleyball	2.3

Example 1

Dale weighs 100 pounds. Each morning, she walks for 25 minutes. How many calories does she use each morning? Use the information in the table.

A. You can use simpler numbers to plan how to solve the problem.

Exact Number	**Simpler Number**
2.7	3

B. Next, use a simpler number to set up the problem.

25 x 3 = _____

Now, you can use the exact number to find the exact answer.

_____ x 2.7 = _____

So, Dale uses _____ calories each morning.

Example 2

Armand weighs 100 pounds. He used 103.5 calories playing volleyball. For how many minutes did he play?

A. Use simpler numbers to set up and solve the problem.

104 ÷ 2 = _____

B. Now, use the exact numbers to find the exact answer.

_____ ÷ _____ = _____

So, Armand played volleyball for _____ minutes.

● Multiplication and Division with Decimals

GUIDED PRACTICE

The table below shows the numbers of calories used during
different exercises by a person who weighs 100 pounds.

1. Aziz weighs 100 pounds. He jogged
   for 15 minutes and then walked for
   12 more minutes. How many
   calories did he use?

   Calories Used During Exercises

Activity	Calories Used Per Minute
walking	2.7
jogging	6.1
volleyball	2.3

   a. Use simpler numbers to help you
      solve the problem.

      For jogging, 6.1 simplifies to 6.

      For walking, _____ simplifies to _____.

   b. Use the simpler numbers to set up and solve the problem.

      15   x _____ = _____ calories

      _____ x _____ = _____ calories

   Add.

      _____ + _____ = _____ calories

   Now, use the exact numbers to find the exact answer.

      15 x _____ = _____ calories

      _____ x _____ = _____ calories

      _____ + _____ = _____ calories

   So, Aziz used _____ calories during his exercise.

2. Aziz pays $2.25 an hour to use the Sports Center. He was there for 3 hours a
   day for 5 days last week. How much did he pay for the week? **Use simpler
   numbers to plan the problem. Then find the exact answer.**

   First, multiply to find how many hours he was there.

      _____ x _____ = _____ hours

   Then, use simpler numbers to solve the problem.

      _____ x _____ = _____ dollars

   Now, use the exact numbers to find the exact answer.

      _____ x _____ = _____ dollars

   So, Aziz paid $ _____ for the week.

PRACTICE

Janira is a buyer for a restaurant. The table below shows the price per pound of various items that she needs to buy for the party. Use the table to solve the problems.

Market Prices

Item	Price Per Pound
Leg of Lamb	$9.83
Iceberg Lettuce	$2.29
New Potatoes	$3.79
T-Bone Steak	$12.32
Pork Chops	$9.03

For problems 3 and 4, use simpler numbers to plan. Then solve exactly.

3. Janira decided to buy an 8-pound leg of lamb. How much will the lamb cost?

_____

_____

The lamb will cost $ _____.

4. Janira paid $16.45 for a 5-pound bag of new potatoes on sale. What was the sale price per pound?

_____

_____

The sale price was $ _____.

Solve . . . .

5. Janira decided to buy 12 pounds of pork chops and 9 pounds of T-bone steak. **How much did Janira pay for these items?**

_____

6. Janira paid $9.45 for 5 pounds of iceberg lettuce on sale. **How much less was the sale price per pound than the regular price per pound?**

_____

7. Just before leaving the market, Janira saw a 9-pound leg of lamb on sale for $80.91. **How much was its price per pound?**

_____

8. Janira decided to buy 4 more pounds of potatoes and 5 more pounds of lettuce at regular prices. **How much did she have to pay?**

_____

TEST-TAKING PRACTICE

Use the information in the table to answer questions 1–4.
Choose the best answer for each problem. In the answer section
at the bottom of this page, fill in the box of your choice.

Swimming Times

Swimmer	Time for One Lap
Chris	23.56 s
Marna	24.77 s
Kathy	21.07 s

1. **Which would be good simpler numbers for the three times?**
   A Chris 23 s, Marna 24 s, Kathy 21 s
   B Chris 23.6 s, Marna 24.8 s, Kathy 21.1 s
   C Chris 23.5 s, Marna 24.7 s, Kathy 21.0 s
   D Chris 24 s, Marna 25 s, Kathy 21 s

2. **Which operation will tell you which swimmer swam 4 laps at lap time in 84.28 s?**
   J Divide each time by 4.
   K Divide 84.28 by each time.
   L Multiply each time by 84.28.
   M Subtract each time from 84.28.

3. **At his lap time, how long would it take Chris to swim 5 laps?**
   A 4.71 s   C 117.8 s
   B 23.56 s   D 120 s

4. **The clock shows 63.21 s. How many laps did Kathy swim?**
   J 21.07 s   L 4
   K 3   M 6

Write About It

Write a plan to solve the problem by using simpler numbers. Then find the exact answer by using the actual numbers from the table. Explain how you found your answers.

5. **Marna and Chris swam laps as a team. They each swam 3 laps. What was their combined time?**

_____

_____

_____

_____

_____

_____

_____

_____

_____

1. A ☐ B ☐ C ☐ D ☐   3. A ☐ B ☐ C ☐ D ☐

2. J ☐ K ☐ L ☐ M ☐   4. J ☐ K ☐ L ☐ M ☐

● Multiplication and Division with Decimals

Underlining Information

Sometimes, you might find it helpful to underline the information you need to solve a problem.

Example 1

Tickets to a football game cost $8 for adults and $5.75 for students. Children under 5 can go for free. What is the cost of 6 student tickets?

A. What is the question that you have to answer?

What is the cost of 6 student tickets?

B. Look at the problem again, and find the information you need to answer the question. Underline the information.

$5.75 for students

C. Use the information that you underlined to answer the question.

6 x 5.75 = _____

So, the cost of 6 student tickets is $ _____.

Example 2

Two of the world's fastest animals are the greyhound and the cheetah. The greyhound is a racing dog and weighs about 65 pounds. The fastest recorded speed of a greyhound is 39.35 miles per hour. The cheetah weighs about 100 pounds and feeds on small deer and antelopes. To catch its prey, a cheetah can reach a speed of 70 miles per hour. Can a cheetah run twice as fast as a greyhound?

Step 1: **Underline the information you need to answer the question.**

Step 2: **Use the information you underlined to answer the question.**

You can use estimation to compare the numbers.

THINK: Round 39.35 to the nearest ten. So, a greyhound can run at about 40 miles per hour.

Find twice the estimated speed of a greyhound. 2 x 40 = _____

Compare the two numbers. 80 _____ 70

Can a cheetah run twice as fast as a greyhound? _____

● Multiplication and Division with Decimals

1. Dominic worked at a video store on Saturday. He sold 23
    videos, rented 85 videos, and 12 laser discs. He earned $26.25
    for 5 hours of work. How much was he paid per hour?

    a. **Underline the information you need to answer the question.**

    b. **Use the information that you underlined to answer the question.**

    _____ ÷ 5 = _____

    So, Dominic was paid $ _____ per hour.

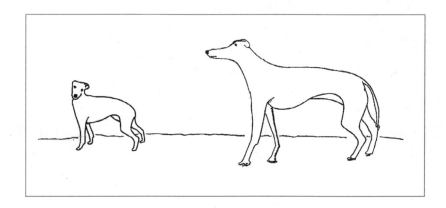

2. The whippet is a dog that looks like a greyhound, but the
    whippet is much smaller. A whippet weighs about 20
    pounds. The fastest recorded speed of a whippet is 35.50
    miles per hour, but whippets are not often raced.
    Greyhounds, on the other hand, are known as racing dogs.
    A greyhound can reach a speed of 39.35 miles per hour.
    How much faster can a greyhound run than a whippet?

    a. **Underline the information you need to answer the question.**

    b. **Use the information that you underlined to answer the question.**

    _____ – 35.50 = _____

    The greyhound can run _____ miles an hour faster than the whippet.

PRACTICE

For problems 3 and 4, underline the information you need.
Then solve.

3. Diana loves animals and researches them as a hobby. She looked up horses in the encyclopedia and found that their top speed is 47.5 miles per hour. The next day she rode her horse 18.5 miles in 2 hours. How many miles did Diana ride per hour?

_____

_____

4. Track is a popular sport at the Chavez School. There are 27 boys and girls on the track team. The team trains on a track that is 0.25 miles around. Each night, the team trains for 2 hours. If the team members run 24 laps, how many miles have they run?

_____

_____

Solve . . . .

5. Talitha and 2 friends share a paper route with 212 customers. This month they received the following tips: $11.89, $9.87, and $8.78. If they share the tips equally, how much money will each person receive?

_____

_____

6. Levar and Andrew are training for a walking race. Levar has been training for 10 months and can walk at 5 miles per hour. Andrew walks at 4 miles per hour. The race is 2 miles long. How long will it take Levar to finish the race?

_____

7. A ferry boat service on Blue Mountain Lake takes passengers across the lake for $6.50 each. Each trip is one-way only. The lake is 3.4 miles across. If the ferry makes 18 trips a day, how many miles does it travel?

_____

_____

8. For a reunion, the Proctor family rented a cottage for $3,000 for one week. Family members also shared the food bill, which came to $489.78. The Proctor family has 5 members. About how much did each person pay for the vacation?

_____

Use the information below for problems 1–3. Choose the best answer for each problem. In the answer section at the bottom of this page, fill in the box of your choice.

A class at Webster School collected data on ball-throwing distances. They found that the average distance a Webster student can throw a ball is 15 yards. Some students can throw the ball much farther, and some can't throw it as far. A student named Henry threw the ball 1.5 times the average throw. Tara threw the ball only 0.75 times the average.

1. How far did Tara throw the ball? **Which information should you underline to help to answer this question?**
   A The students at Webster School collected data on ball-throwing distances.
   B The average student at Webster School can throw a ball 15 yards.
   C Some students can throw the ball much farther.
   D Henry threw the ball 1.5 times the average throw.

2. **How far did Henry throw the ball?**
   J 1.5 yd   L 22.5 yd
   K 15 yd   M 225 yd

3. **If Jenna threw the ball 3.2 yards farther than 15 yards, how far did she throw it?**
   A 3.2 yd   C 18.2 yd
   B 15 yd   D 48 yd

Write About It

In the problem below, underline the information you need to answer it. Explain why you didn't underline some of the information. Then solve.

4. Boise, Idaho, whose metropolitan area is 1,060 square miles, has an average daily high temperature in January of 36.4°F. Honolulu, Hawaii, whose metropolitan area is 621 square miles, has an average daily high temperature in January of 80.1°F. **Is Honolulu's average daily high temperature in January more than twice that of Boise's?**

_____

_____

_____

_____

_____

_____

_____

1. A ☐ B ☐ C ☐ D ☐   3. A ☐ B ☐ C ☐ D ☐

2. J ☐ K ☐ L ☐ M ☐

● Multiplication and Division with Decimals

Interpreting the Quotient

Carefully reading the question in a division problem will help you decide on the kind of answer you need and how to interpret the quotient.

Here are three problems you can solve with the same number sentence.

1. The workers at a factory take 18 seconds to stamp a logo on each product. How many logos can they stamp on products in 45 seconds?

2. A shuttle-bus service takes people from a hotel to a train station. Each bus can carry 18 people. One day, 45 people are waiting to take the shuttle. How many buses are needed?

3. Zane is organizing a camping trip. He needs 18 short pieces of rope of equal length to set up the tents. He has 1 piece of rope that is 45 feet long. If he cuts the rope into 18 equal pieces, how long will each piece be?

You can use this number sentence for each problem:

$$45 \div 18 = 2.5$$

The numbers are the same, but they mean something different in each problem.

	45	÷ 18	= 2.5
1.	Total time	Time per logo	The workers can stamp on 2.5 logos in 45 seconds.
2.	People waiting	People per bus	To take 45 people, 2.5 buses are needed.
3.	Length of rope	Pieces of rope	Zane can cut 45 feet of rope into 18 pieces 2.5 feet long.

Problem 1: Because it does not make sense to stamp on only part of a logo, the answer to the question is _____ logos.

Problem 2: Because the answer "2.5 buses" does not make sense, the answer to the question is _____ buses.

Problem 3: Because 2.5 feet is a measurement, the answer to the question is _____ feet.

● Division with Decimals

GUIDED PRACTICE

Complete each chart to answer each problem.

Problem-Solving Tips:
To solve a division problem whose quotient is a decimal, you may need to
- round down to the nearest whole number.
- round up to the nearest whole number.
- use the exact answer.

1. Jose coaches an elementary school soccer team. The team has a budget of $450 for jerseys. Each jersey costs $40. How many jerseys can Jose buy?

450   ÷   40   =   _____

Team budget	Cost of jersey	Number of jerseys Jose can buy

What does the quotient mean?

_____

So, Jose can buy _____ jerseys.

2. Tanya is hiking a trail that is 450 kilometers long. Each day, she hikes 40 kilometers. How many days will it take Tanya to hike the entire trail?

450   ÷   _____   =   _____

	Kilometers Tanya hikes each day	Number of days Tanya hikes

What does the quotient mean?

_____

So, it will take _____ days for Tanya to hike the trail.

3. Kim makes earrings and sells them to jewelry stores. One store orders 40 pairs of earrings for a total of $450. What is the cost to the store for 1 pair of earrings?

450   ÷   40   =   _____

		Cost of one pair of earrings

So, the cost to the store for 1 pair of earrings is $ _____.

PRACTICE

For each problem, tell what the quotient means. Then complete the answer.

4. Stevie is planning a family reunion. He needs to find out how many picnic tables he will need. He expects 46 people to attend. Each picnic table seats 8 people. How many picnic tables will Stevie need?

   What does the quotient mean?

   _____

   _____

   So, Stevie will need _____ picnic tables.

5. Eight friends decide to share a large order of chicken wings. A large order has 53 wings. They decide to share the wings evenly and save whatever is left for a ninth friend who's coming later. How many wings can each of the 8 friends have?

   What does the quotient mean?

   _____

   _____

   So, each of the 8 friends can have

   _____ chicken wings.

Solve . . . .

6. Ancient Romans measured length using a unit called a *cubit*. A Roman cubit is 17.5 inches long. **About how many feet are there in 1 cubit?**

   _____

7. Aza is planning a canoe trip for 25 people. Each canoe can hold 2 people. **How many canoes will Aza need?**

   _____

8. Siva makes computers. Each computer has 36 chips in it. **If Siva has 306 computer chips, how many computers can she make?**

9. Esmerelda buys 4 CDs for $25. **If each CD costs the same amount of money, how much does 1 CD cost?**

   _____

10. In a video game, Bernardo races a car around a track 5 times. His total time is 3 minutes and 26 seconds. **To a tenth of a second, what is his average time per lap?**

    _____

11. Ryan is recording some songs. **If each song is 2 minutes and 30 seconds long, how many songs can Ryan record on a 60-minute tape?**

    _____

TEST-TAKING PRACTICE

Choose the best answer for each problem. Then in the answer section at the bottom of this page, fill in the box of your choice.

1. A town baseball league is going to the So Much Fun amusement park. It will cost $11 for each person to go. The league has 484 people in it. If each bus seats 40 people, how many buses will the league need?

    What does the decimal in the quotient mean in this problem?

    A Some people will not go to the amusement park.

    B Some people will go to the amusement park on a bus that is not full.

    C A fraction of a bus will go to the amusement park.

    D The amount of change each person will get if he or she pays with a $20 bill.

2. Darlene is organizing a running race. The course is 8 miles long. She wants to break the race up into 5 equal sections.

    To the nearest tenth of a mile, how long is each section of the race?

    J 1.0 mile   L 1.6 miles
    K 1 R2 miles   M 2.0 miles

3. Dale makes model cars. He needs 5 wheels for each car because each has a spare tire.

    If Dale has 153 wheels, how many cars can he make?

    A 30   C 30.6
    B 30 R2   D 31

4. Juan is the captain of the chess club at his school. He has to buy chess sets for the chess club with money from the school budget. With $250.00, he buys 14 sets.

    How much does each set cost?

    J $17   L $17.80
    K 17 R12   M Not given

Write About It

5. At the store, Mark wants to buy as many grapes as he can with $18.60. Grapes cost $2.00 a pound. To the nearest tenth of a pound, how many pounds can Mark buy?

    Find the quotient. What does the decimal stand for? Do you need to round? Solve.

    _____

    _____

    _____

    _____

1. A ☐ B ☐ C ☐ D ☐   3. A ☐ B ☐ C ☐ D ☐
2. J ☐ K ☐ L ☐ M ☐   4. J ☐ K ☐ L ☐ M ☐

● Division with Decimals

Which Answer Makes Sense?

Deciding on the kind of answer you need will help you to solve problems. Sometimes, you have to decide whether or not you need to round your answer.

Example 1

Sang wants to send gift cards to some of his family members who live in Korea. He has $15.00 to spend. The gift cards he likes cost $4.00 each. How many cards can Sang buy?

A. You want to know how many gift cards Sang can buy with $15.00. You can divide $15.00 by $4.00 to find the answer.

$$15.00 \div 4.00 = 3.75$$

B. Look at the question you need to answer:

How many cards can Sang buy?

Notice that the question asks <u>how many</u> cards rather than <u>how much</u> something costs.

The number 3.75 tells you that $15.00 is enough money for more than 3 gift cards but not enough for 4. You cannot buy a part of a card. You need to round the number down to 3.

So, Sang can buy 3 cards.

Example 2

Sang finds 9 postcards that he likes and buys them. Each postcard costs $0.75. What is the total cost of the postcards?

Step 1: You know that each postcard costs $0.75 and that Sang buys 9 cards. You can multiply to find the total cost.

$$9 \times 0.75 = 6.75$$

Step 2: Look at the question you need to answer:

What is the total cost of the postcards?

The answer should be a money amount. You do not need to round it because you can write money amounts with two decimal places.

So, the total cost of the postcards is $ _____ .

● Multiplying and Dividing with Money

Use the prices in the window display to solve each problem.

1. A 1-pound bag of apples contains 4 apples. Alexa wants to buy only one apple. What would be the cost of one apple?

   a. You want to know the cost of one apple when 4 apples cost $1.10. You can divide.

   $$1.10 \div \underline{\hspace{2cm}} = 0.275$$

   b. Decide on the kind of answer you need.

   ....
   : Note: Stores :
   : always round :
   : up 0.5. :
   ....

   Should the answer be a money amount? _____

   Does 0.275 answer the question? _____

   Does the answer need to be rounded to make sense? _____

   What is the answer that makes sense? $ _____

   So, one apple costs $ _____.

2. Delia needs to buy chicken for a barbecue. She has $13.50 to spend. How many pounds of chicken can she buy?

   a. You want to know how many times $2.00 goes into $13.50. You can divide.

   $$\underline{\hspace{2cm}} \div \underline{\hspace{2cm}} = 6.75$$

   b. Decide on the kind of answer you need.

   Should the answer be a money amount? _____

   Should the answer be rounded? _____

   What is the answer that makes sense? _____ pounds of chicken

   So, Delia can buy _____ pounds of chicken.

Name _____

PRACTICE

For problems 3 and 4, write whether each answer should be a money amount and whether it should be rounded. Then solve.

3. Mr. Bertram wants to rent a car to visit his relatives in Boston. The car rental company charges $49.98 per day. The trip will last 3 days. How much will it cost to rent the car?

4. Gillian wants to see a movie. A regular ticket costs $3.75. The theater is offering half-price tickets for the weekday matinee. How much will a matinee ticket cost?

_____

_____

It will cost Mr. Bertram

$ _____ to rent the car for 3 days.

_____

_____

A matinee ticket will cost

_____.

Solve . . . .

5. A bicycle race is divided into 5 legs. Each leg is 4.65 miles long. **What is the total length of the race?**

7. Joplin works at a bakery. In 8 hours, she bakes 420 rolls. **To the nearest 10 rolls, about how many rolls does she bake each hour?**

_____

_____

6. Jorge likes to make model airplanes. He has $100.00, and each model kit costs $12.98. Jorge calculates this answer: 7.70. **How many model kits can he buy?**

8. Fiona spends a lot of time on the Internet. She pays $29.78 a month for her Internet service. **How much does she spend for Internet service for a year?**

_____

_____

● Multiplying and Dividing with Money

TEST-TAKING PRACTICE

Choose the best answer for each problem. In the answer section at the bottom of this page, fill in the box of your choice.

Use the information in the table to answer questions 1-4.

Prices at Sports City

Item	Price
running shoes	$37.55
sweat socks	$1.29
sweat pants	$21.90
sweat shirt	$9.00

1. Renata wants to buy a sweat shirt for each of her 3 children.
   How much must she spend to buy the sweat shirts?

   A $9.00   C $27.00
   B $18.00   D $36.00

2. Malcolm wants to buy sweat pants for his soccer team.
   How many pairs of sweat pants can he buy with $350.00?

   J 15   L 15.98
   K $15.98   M 16

3. Frank wants to buy matching sweat pants and sweat shirts for the 9 members of his baseball team.
   How much must he spend to buy the sets of sweat pants and sweat shirts?

   A $30.90   C $300.90
   B $278.10   D $378.10

Write About It

Write a plan for solving the problem. Will the answer be a money amount? Will you need to round? Solve.

4. **Mrs. Jenkins wants to buy a pair of running shoes and a pair of socks for each of her grandchildren. If she has $250.00, how many sets of shoes and socks can she buy.**

   _____

   _____

   _____

   _____

   _____

   _____

   _____

---

1. A ☐ B ☐ C ☐ D ☐   3. A ☐ B ☐ C ☐ D ☐

2. J ☐ K ☐ L ☐ M ☐

● Multiplying and Dividing with Money

Solving Multi-Step Problems

Sometimes, you may need to take three or more steps to solve a problem. To solve such problems, it is helpful to decide what you can find first.

Example

The town council is having a bake sale. So far, the council has sold 9 brownies for $0.50 each and 14 cookies for $0.35 each. How much has the council earned so far?

A. You need to find the total earned. You can write a word equation to show the problem.

| **Money earned selling brownies** | + | **Money earned selling cookies** | = | **Total earned** |

B. Look at the word equation. Decide what you can find first.

Before you add, you have to know which numbers to add.

To find the numbers, first find out how much the council earned selling brownies and how much the council earned selling cookies.

Money earned selling brownies = 9   x 0.50   → $ _____

Money earned selling cookies   = 14 x _____ → $ _____

C. Put the numbers you found into the word equation you wrote. Then solve.

Money earned selling brownies	+	**Money earned selling cookies**	=	**Total earned**
↓		↓		↓
_____	+	_____	=	$ _____

So, the town council has earned $ _____ so far.

GUIDED PRACTICE

1. At the bake sale, Christie buys 3 cookies and 2 brownies. She pays with a $5 bill. What change should she receive?

   Step 1: Write a word equation to find Christie's change from a $5 bill.

   $5 – Amount spent = _____

   Step 2: Write a word equation to find the amount spent.

   Cost of 2 brownies + _____ = **Amount spent**

   Step 3: Find the numbers to put in the word equation.

   Cost of 2 brownies   +   Cost of 3 cookies   =   _____

   ↓   ↓   ↓

   $1.00   + $ _____   = $ _____

   **Step 4: Look at the first word equation.
   Write the numbers you now know in the equation. Then solve.**

   $ _____   –   **Amount spent**   =   **Christie's change**

   ↓   ↓   ↓

   $ _____   – $ _____   = $ _____

   So, Christie gets $ _____ in change from a $5 bill.

2. The head baker estimated that each brownie cost $0.20 to make. By the end of the day, the town council had sold 245 brownies at $0.50 each. How much did the council make on brownies?

   Step 1: Write a word equation to find the profit made selling brownies.

   Amount made   –   _____   =   _____

   selling brownies   _____   _____

   **Step 2: Write word equations to find numbers for the first word equation.
   Then solve.**

   _____

   _____

   _____

   So, the town council made $ _____ on brownies.

PRACTICE

For problems 3 and 4, write word equations to help you decide what to do first and how to solve the problem. Then solve.

3. The town soccer team sold pizzas to raise money. The team members sold 24 cheese pizzas at $11.50 each and 37 sausage pizzas at $13.75 each. What was the total earned?

   Word equations:

   _____

   _____

   _____

   _____

   _____

   The total earned was $ _____ .

4. Jordan bought 7 pizzas for $11.50 each and 4 pizzas for $13.75 each. He gave the delivery person $140. What change should he receive?

   Word equations:

   _____

   _____

   _____

   _____

   _____

   Jordan should receive $ _____ .

Solve . . . .

5. The pizza company can make 12 pizzas an hour. If the company makes pizzas for 8 hours, its costs are $395.52. **How much does it cost the company to make one pizza?**

   _____

   _____

   _____

6. The swim team sold 87 pizzas for a total of $1,095. The team can keep $3.50 for each pizza. The rest of the money is paid to the pizza company. **How much money does the team owe the pizza company?**

   _____

   _____

   _____

• Multiplication and Division with Decimals

TEST-TAKING PRACTICE

Choose the best answer for each problem. In the answer section at the bottom of the page, fill in the box of your choice.

1. Bella bought 12 roses for $1.50 each and 18 carnations for $0.98 each. She gave the flower shop $40. What change should she receive?

   Which equation could help you decide what to do first in this problem?

   A $40 – the total cost of the flowers = the change Bella should receive.

   B 12 x 1.50 = the change Bella should receive.

   C 18 + 12 = $30 + the change Bella should receive.

   D $40 – the cost of one flower = the change Bella should receive.

2. **Anne worked for three hours. Her pay was three $5 bills, two $1 bills, and one quarter. How much did she earn per hour?**

   J $5.50   L $15.75
   K $5.75   M $17.75

3. **Kinte bought 2 shirts for $9.95 each, 1 pair of pants for $25.99, and 4 pairs of socks for $3.49 each. How much did he spend?**

   A $19.90   C $49.38
   B $45.89   D $59.85

4. **Zoe sold 37 posters for $8.95 each, 18 photographs for $5.00 each, and 20 postcards for $0.25 each. What is the total of her sales?**

   J $331.15   L $426.15
   K $421.15   M $471.15

Write About It

Write a plan for solving the following problem. Then solve.

5. **Vinnie rents 3 video games at $3.59 each and 2 movies at $2.95 each. He gives the clerk a $20 bill. How much change should he receive?**

   _____

   _____

   _____

   _____

   _____

   _____

   _____

1. A ☐ B ☐ C ☐ D ☐   3. A ☐ B ☐ C ☐ D ☐
2. J ☐ K ☐ L ☐ M ☐   4. J ☐ K ☐ L ☐ M ☐

● Multiplication and Division with Decimals

Writing an Equivalent Problem

Showing the information in a problem in a different way can sometimes help you solve the problem. One way of doing this is to write an equivalent problem.

Example 1

Community theater members sold dried fruit for $3 per pound. They earned a total of $813.75. How many pounds of dried fruit did they sell?

A. You can write a word equation that shows the problem's information.

Total money earned = Dollars per pound x Number of pounds

B. You can write an equivalent division equation from the first equation. The question asks how many pounds the theater sold. So, you need to write an equation for the **number of pounds.**

Total money earned ÷ Dollars per pound = _____

C. Write the numbers you know into the equation, and then solve.

813.75 ÷ _____ = _____ pounds

So, the community theater sold _____ pounds of dried fruit.

Example 2

Roxanne is a goalie on the local hockey team. She makes an average of 12.5 saves per game. If the team played 26 games in the season, how many total saves did Roxanne make?

Step 1: You can write a word equation that shows the problem's information.

Average saves per game = _____ ÷ Number of games

Step 2: You can write an equivalent multiplication equation from the equation above. The question asks how many total saves Roxanne made. So, you need to write an equation for the **total saves.**

_____ x _____ = Total saves

Step 3: Write the numbers you know into the equation, and then solve.

26 x _____ = _____ saves

So, Roxanne made a total of _____ saves.

• Multiplication and Division with Decimals

1. A group of Boy Scouts sold baseball caps for $3.00 each at the city softball championships. They earned a total of $870.00. How many baseball caps did they sell?

   a. **Write a word equation that shows the problem's information.**

   Total money earned = _____ **x** _____

   b. **Write an equivalent division equation for the number of caps sold.**

   _____ **÷** _____ **= Number of caps sold**

   c. **Write the numbers you know into the equation, and then solve.**

   _____ **÷** _____ **=** _____ **caps sold**

   So, the Boy Scouts sold a total of _____ **baseball caps.**

2. Elisa is on a community basketball team. She scores an average of 13.2 points a game. If there are 15 games in a season, about how many total points does she score in a season?

   a. **Write a word equation that shows the problem's information.**

   Average points per game = _____ **÷** _____

   b. **For this problem, you can write an equivalent division equation for the**

   _____ **in a season.**

   _____ **x** _____ **= Total points**

   c. **Write the numbers you know into the equation, and then solve.**

   15 x _____ **=** _____ **points**

   So, Elisa scored a season total of about _____ **points.**

PRACTICE

For problems 3 and 4, write a word equation showing each problem's information. Then write an equivalent word equation for solving each problem, and solve.

3. Enrique buys 15 pounds of ground beef for a dinner party. He pays a total of $36.75 for the ground beef. **What is the cost per pound of the ground beef?**

_____

_____

_____

_____

So, the cost per pound of ground

beef is $ _____ .

4. Enrique also buys cheese pies to serve as dessert at his dinner party. **If he pays a total of $20.45, and he buys 5 cheese pies, what is the cost of each cheese pie?**

_____

_____

_____

_____

So, the cost of each cheese pie is

$ _____ .

Solve . . . .

5. It takes a machine in a factory 25.6 minutes to stamp 16 records. **How many minutes does it take the machine to stamp one record?**

_____

_____

6. Jenny's favorite chicken lays an average of 3.6 eggs a week. **In a period of 15 weeks, about how many eggs will the chicken lay?**

_____

_____

7. Jorge prints and sells his own photos. One day, he sells 4 equally priced photos for a total of $568.20. **How much does one photo cost?**

_____

_____

8. Josh spends 2.8 hours a day talking on the phone. **In 21 days, how many hours does Josh spend talking on the phone?**

_____

_____

● Multiplication and Division with Decimals

TEST-TAKING PRACTICE

Choose the best answer for each problem. In the answer section at the bottom of this page, fill in the box of your choice.

1. Margaret and Tim are planning their wedding dinner. They plan on 75 guests. The total cost for the dinner is $3,975. What is the cost for each guest?

   Which word equation would help you solve this problem?

   A Total cost of dinner x Cost for each guest = 75

   B Total cost of dinner ÷ Number of guests = Cost for each guest

   C Total cost of dinner = Number of guests ÷ 75

   D Number of guests ÷ Total cost = Cost for each guest

2. **Jon and Ki invite 87 guests to their wedding. The cost for each guest is $12.67. What is the total cost of the wedding?**

   J $1,102.29   L $2,897.51
   K $2,008.49   M $6,567.77

3. **Bryan and Sabina spent $750.00 for wedding flowers. The cost per flower was $2.00. How many flowers did they buy?**

   A 3.75   C 375
   B 37.5   D 3,750

4. **Ed and Marcia invite 138 guests to their wedding. If the cost for each guest is $18.33, how much do they spend in total?**

   J $2,529.54   L $4,284,94
   K $3,899.83   M $6,452.89

Write About It

Write an equation for the information in the problem. Then write an equivalent equation for solving the problem, and solve.

5. **Sharon and Jeremy go on a cruise for their honeymoon. The cruise costs $2,072.98 and lasts for 14 days. What is the cost of one day of the cruise?**

_____

_____

_____

_____

_____

_____

1. A☐ B☐ C☐ D☐   3. A☐ B☐ C☐ D☐
2. J☐ K☐ L☐ M☐   4. J☐ K☐ L☐ M☐

© 1999 Metropolitan Teaching & Learning Co.

58   • Multiplication and Division with Decimals

Organizing a List

Sometimes, you have to use a large amount of data to solve a problem. You can show the information in another way and organize it into a list.

Example

The table below lists the numbers of tickets sold for performances of a play. Find the mode and the median of ticket sales for the performances.

Tickets Sold for "The Trapped Mouse"

1/11	1/12	1/13	1/15	1/16	1/17	1/18	1/19	1/20	1/22	1/23	1/24	1/26	1/27	1/28
84	88	45	48	52	50	64	74	80	48	52	43	52	83	88

A. You'll find it helpful to list the ticket sales in order.

Step 1: First, find the least number. Read the table from left to right, and underline any number that you think may be the smallest one.

The first number I'll underline is 45.

Step 2: Keep reading. As you find other small numbers, compare each to the underlined number. Underline a new number if you need to.

I'll underline 43 and erase the line under 45.

Step 3: When you've finished reading the table, you'll have found the least number. Begin your list.

The least number in the list is 43. I'll cross it out in the table.

Step 4: Repeat the process to find the next smallest number in the table. Some numbers may appear more than once. Make sure you list each number as many times as it appears.

List the ticket sales in order from least to greatest.

43, 45, 48, 48, 50, 52, 52, 52, 64, 74, 80, 83, 84, 88, 88

B. **Find the most frequent number in your organized list.**

The number _____ appears three times. **So, the mode is _____.**

Find the middle number in your organized list.

The eighth number on the list is _____. **So, the median is _____.**

The table below lists the average monthly rainfall in Honolulu, Hawaii.

Honolulu's Average Monthly Rainfall, in Inches

Jan	Feb	Mar	Apr	May	Jun	Jul	Aug	Sep	Oct	Nov	Dec
3.6	2.2	2.2	1.5	1.1	0.5	0.6	0.4	0.8	2.3	3.0	3.8

1. What is the range of Honolulu's monthly rainfall?

    a. Write the information in order from least to greatest rainfall.

    _____

    b. What are the first and last numbers on your list? _____ and _____

    c. Find the difference between the numbers. 3.8 – 0.4 = _____

    So, the range is _____ inches.

2. Use the table to find the median high temperature during the week.

    a. Write the numbers in an ordered list.

    _____

    b. Find the middle number in the list.

    The fourth number is _____

    So, the median temperature is _____°C.

    ### Daily High Temperature

Sunday	−4°C
Monday	−5°C
Tuesday	−2°C
Wednesday	3°C
Thursday	5°C
Friday	−1°C
Saturday	1°C

3. Organizing data into a list can help you solve problems.

    a. How does organizing data help to find the range of a set of numbers?

    _____

    b. How does organizing data help to find the median of a set of numbers?

    _____

Name_____

PRACTICE

The table below gives the high temperature recorded in Chicago, Illinois, on each day for one week.

Temperature in Chicago, Illinois

Day	High Temperature
Sunday	62°F
Monday	65°F
Tuesday	59°F
Wednesday	62°F
Thursday	67°F
Friday	70°F
Saturday	71°F

4. What is the order of temperatures from lowest to highest?

_____

5. On how many days was the temperature higher than 66°F?

_____

6. What is the lowest temperature for the week?

_____

7. On how many days was the high temperature lower than 70°F?

_____

8. What is the highest temperature for the week?

_____

9. What is the mode of the high temperatures for the week?

_____

10. What is the range of the high temperatures for the week?

_____

11. What is the median high temperature for the week?

_____

● Using Statistical Measures

Use the table to choose the best answer for problems 1–6. In the answer section at the bottom of the page, fill in the box of your choice.

Daily Attendance at Reptile World

Sunday	Monday	Tuesday	Wednesday	Thursday	Friday	Saturday
88	43	52	55	52	67	83

1. **Which set of numbers lists the attendance in order from least to greatest?**

   A 43, 52, 55, 67, 83, 88
   B 43, 52, 52, 55, 67, 83, 88
   C 88, 83, 67, 55, 52, 52, 43
   D 88, 43, 52, 55, 52, 67, 83, 88

2. **On how many days did more than 70 people visit Reptile World?**

   J 3 days   L 5 days
   K 4 days   M 2 days

3. **If attendance on Saturday increased by 2, what would happen to the range?**

   A It would increase by 2.
   B It would decrease by 2.
   C It would double.
   D It would stay the same.

4. **What is the median of the daily attendance figures at Reptile World?**

   J 43   L 55
   K 52   M 88

5. **How would you find the range of attendance at Reptile World?**

   A Add the lowest number to the highest number.
   B Add the lowest number to the highest, and divide by 2.
   C Choose the middle number in the list.
   D Subtract the lowest number from the highest number.

6. **What is the mode of the daily attendance figures at Reptile World?**

   J 43   L 55
   K 52   M 88

Write About It

7. **Why is it helpful to organize data into an ordered list to find the median of the data?**

   _____

   _____

   _____

   _____

1. A ☐ B ☐ C ☐ D ☐   4. J ☐ K ☐ L ☐ M ☐

2. J ☐ K ☐ L ☐ M ☐   5. A ☐ B ☐ C ☐ D ☐

3. A ☐ B ☐ C ☐ D ☐   6. J ☐ K ☐ L ☐ M ☐

● Using Statistical Measures

Reading a Line Graph

The information that you need to solve a problem may be presented in a line graph. Line graphs are often used to show a change over time.

The graph at the right shows the daily high temperature for one week in January. The horizontal axis of a line graph usually shows time intervals. On this graph, the horizontal axis shows the date for each temperature reading. The vertical axis on the graph shows the high temperature reading for each day.

Example

What was the high temperature on January 10?

A. Find the value of each interval on the vertical axis. Use a finger to count the number of intervals between 0° and 10°.

> **Divide the range, which is 10°, by the number of intervals.**
>
> 10 ÷ _____ = _____. **So, each interval represents 2°.**

B. Look for the point plotted directly above 1/10 on the horizontal axis. Run your finger along the grid lines from the point. Mark the corresponding place on the vertical axis with a pencil, and write in the value of the grid line. If the point is between two grid lines, mark the values of both.

> **Which values is the point halfway between?**
>
> _____
>
> **So, the high temperature was _____.**

GUIDED PRACTICE
Use the line graph at the right to find the information you need to solve the problems.

Daily High Temperature

1. On which two days was the temperature the lowest?

   a. Look for the two lowest points on the graph— the points closest to the horizontal axis. Run your finger downward from each of the two points to the horizontal axis.

      What dates do the two points correspond to on the horizontal axis?

      _____ and _____

   b. So, the temperature was lowest on

      _____ and _____.

   > Notice that this graph has a break at the bottom—the temperatures begin at 30°F. The break lets you know that there are no readings between 0°F and 30°F.

2. How many degrees did the temperature change between March 5 and March 6?

   a. Find the value of the intervals on the vertical axis.

      How many degrees does each interval represent?

      _____ degrees

   b. Look for points directly above 3/5 and 3/6 on the horizontal axis. Run your finger from those two points to the vertical axis.

      What values do the two points have on the vertical axis?

      _____ and _____

   c. Subtract to find the temperature change.

      What is the difference between the two readings?

      _____ degrees

      So, the temperature changed _____ degrees.

Name _____

PRACTICE

Use the line graph to find the information you need to solve the problems.

3. **How many bushels per acre of soybeans were produced in 1987?**

   _____

4. **In which year was soybean production the lowest?**

   _____

5. **In which two years was the production of soybeans the same?**

   _____

6. **By how much did soybean production decrease between 1987 and 1988?**

   _____

The graph shows annual production of soybeans in the United States for the years 1985 through 1990. The production is given in bushels per acre.

U.S. Soybean Production

Solve . . . .

7. **In how many years was soybean production greater than 32 bushels per acre? Which years were they?**

   _____

8. **Between which two years was there the greatest change in soybean production?**

   _____

9. **How many more bushels per acre were produced in 1990 than in 1988?**

   _____

10. **Between which two years was there the least change in soybean production? What was the change?**

   _____

● Multiplication

Choose the best answer for each problem. In the answer section at the bottom of the page, fill in the box of your choice.

Gas Prices at Rob's Garage

1. What does the graph show?

A the average monthly price per liter of gasoline

B the average yearly price per liter of gasoline

C the average monthly price per gallon of gasoline

D the average yearly price per gallon of gasoline

2. What was the price per gallon of gasoline in July?

J $1.13   L $1.23

K $1.16   M $1.17

3. Which choice correctly describes the change in gasoline prices from May to June?

A an increase from $1.13 to $1.15

B a decrease from $1.23 to $1.19

C an increase from $1.13 to $1.23

D They remained the same.

4. If you had bought 10 gallons of gasoline at Rob's Garage in April, how much would you have paid?

J $11.30   L $11.50

K $12.30   M $11.20

5. Which choice correctly describes the change in gasoline prices from March to April?

A They increased by 3 cents.

B They decreased by 3 cents.

C They decreased by 2 cents.

D They remained the same.

6. What was the overall change in the price of a gallon of gasoline from March to July?

J It dropped by 5 cents.

K It increased by 5 cents.

L It lasted for 4 months.

M Not given

Write About It

7. Explain why there is a break in the vertical axis of the graph between 0 and $1.10.

_____

_____

1. A ☐ B ☐ C ☐ D ☐   4. J ☐ K ☐ L ☐ M ☐

2. J ☐ K ☐ L ☐ M ☐   5. A ☐ B ☐ C ☐ D ☐

3. A ☐ B ☐ C ☐ D ☐   6. J ☐ K ☐ L ☐ M ☐

● Multiplication

Interpreting Changes in a Line Graph

The direction and steepness of the lines connecting the points in a line graph can provide the information you need to solve a problem.

- A horizontal line shows no change.

- A line sloping upward shows an increase.

- A line sloping downward shows a decrease.

Carla's Savings at the Beginning of Each Month

So, the line sloping upward between November 1 and December 1 shows that Carla's savings increased during November.

Example 1

In which months did Carla's savings decrease?

A. Look for lines in the graph that slope downward.

B. Find the months on the horizontal axis that correspond to those lines.

In which months does the line slope downward?

_____ and _____

So, Carla's savings decreased in _____

and _____ .

Example 2

In which month did Carla's savings stay the same?

Step 1: Look for a line in the graph that has no slope.

Step 2: Find the month on the horizontal axis that corresponds to that line. In which month is the line horizontal?

_____

So, Carla's savings stayed the same in _____ .

• Comparing and Ordering

GUIDED PRACTICE

Use the line graph of Carla's savings to find the information you need to solve the problems.

Carla's Savings at the Beginning of Each Month

The slope of a line can tell you how great the change is over a time interval. The steeper the line, the greater the change.

1. Did Carla's savings decrease more during September or during October?

   a. Find the lines that correspond to September and October. Compare the slopes of the two lines.

   Which of the two lines has the steeper downward slope?

   the line for _____

   b. So, Carla's savings decreased more during _____.

2. During which months did Carla's savings increase by the same amount?

   a. Find the lines in the graph that slope upward. Compare the steepness of the slopes of those lines.

   Which lines slope upward with the same steepness?

   the lines for _____ and _____

   b. So, Carla's savings increased by the same

   amount during _____ and _____.

3. Did Carla save more during July or August?

   a. Find the lines that correspond to July and August. Compare the slope of the two lines.

   Which of the two lines has the steeper upward slope?

   the line for _____

   b. So, Carla saved more during _____.

PRACTICE

Use the line graph to find the information you need
to solve the problems.

4. **Between which two dates
   did the population of
   Juniper Island stay the same?**

   The graph shows the population of
   Juniper Island over a five-year period.

   _____

5. **Did the population of
   Juniper Island increase or
   decrease during 1996?**

   _____

6. **During which year did the
   population of Juniper Island
   decrease?**

   _____

Population of Juniper Island,
1994–1999

Solve . . . .

To solve these problems you may mark or draw on the graph.

7. **Did the population increase
   more during 1994 or during 1996?**

   _____

8. **During which two years was the
   increase in the population the
   same?**

   _____

9. **During which year was there the
   greatest increase in the
   population of Juniper Island?**

   _____

10. **Did the population of Juniper
    Island increase, decrease, or stay
    the same for the period shown
    on the graph?**

    _____

● Comparing and Ordering

Use the graph to choose the best answer for each problem. In the answer section at the bottom of the page, fill in the box of your choice.

Number of Cattle at the Oak–A Ranch

1. **Which statement best describes the overall change in the number of cattle at the ranch between April 1 and October 1?**

   A The number increased.
   B The number decreased.
   C The number stayed the same.
   D You can't tell from the graph.

2. **How did the number of cattle change during June?**

   J It increased.
   K It decreased.
   L 70 cows
   M It stayed the same.

3. **Which months show the same decrease in the number of cattle?**

   A April and August
   B April and September
   C May and July
   D May and June

4. **When did the greatest decrease in the number of cattle over one month take place?**

   J during August
   K during April
   L during September
   M during July

5. **Which statement best describes the change in the number of cattle between April 1 and June 1?**

   A It stayed the same and then dropped.
   B It dropped and then stayed the same.
   C It increased and then dropped.
   D It dropped and then increased.

Write About It

6. **Can you use the graph to find out how many cattle there were at the ranch in the middle of each month? Explain.**

   _____

   _____

   _____

1. A ☐ B ☐ C ☐ D ☐   4. J ☐ K ☐ L ☐ M ☐

2. J ☐ K ☐ L ☐ M ☐   5. A ☐ B ☐ C ☐ D ☐

3. A ☐ B ☐ C ☐ D ☐

© 1999 Metropolitan Teaching & Learning Co.

• Comparing and Ordering

Finding Data in a News Article

Sometimes, the information required to solve a problem is in a newspaper article. You can underline information that you need.

Page 1
Burton Computers Announces Record Sales Month
by Thom Barrett

Burton City, December 10 – Burton Computers, Burton City's leading computer software store, is a very busy place these days. Lois Halbert, the store manager, calls last month's sales "the best ever."

"In November, we sold 60 copies of *Astro Rider*, 45 copies of *Ocean Adventure*, and 27 copies of *Math Wizard*," said Halbert. "Of course, November is usually

---

a good month for sales. But this was the best ever," she added.

The popular *Math Wizard* educational software sells for $12.50, while the *Astro Rider* and *Ocean Adventure* games each sell for $8.75.

Burton Computers also introduced the new software package *Hills and Thrills* in late November. "We sold 21 copies of *Hills and Thrills* the first week it was out," said Halbert. "We expect it to be our leading software seller by early next year."

Continued on Page 2

Example

How much money did Burton Computers take in from November sales of *Ocean Adventure*?

Step 1: Read the problem carefully.

What information do you need to solve the problem?

the _____ of copies of *Ocean Adventure* sold, and the

_____ of each copy

Step 2: Reread the article. Underline the information you need as you read.

How many copies of *Ocean Adventure* were sold? _____

What is the price of each copy of *Ocean Adventure*? _____

Step 3: Multiply to solve the problem.

What is the product of the number of sales and the price?

_____ x _____ = _____

So, Burton Computers took in

$ _____ from November

sales of *Ocean Adventure*.

GUIDED PRACTICE

Use the continuation of the article, below, to answer the questions.

continued from page 1 "Of course, *Astro Rider* has been our best-selling software package for the last year," explained Ms. Halbert. "We are very pleased about that, because it's fun and educational. The game teaches a lot of fun things about space." Ms. Halbert	went on to say that July sales of *Astro Rider* amounted to 22 copies; August and September sales totaled 47 copies each month; 39 copies were sold in October, and 60 copies in November. "That's a great sales record in any store," said Ms. Halbert.

1. How many more copies of *Astro Rider* were sold in August than in July?

   Step 1: Read the problem.

   What information do you need to solve the problem?

   the number of copies sold in

   _____ and in _____ .

   Step 2: Reread the article, underlining the needed information.

   How many copies were sold in August?

   _____

   How many copies were sold in July?

   _____

   Step 3: **Subtract to solve the problem.**

   _____ − _____ = _____

   So, _____ more copies were sold in August than in July.

2. For problem 2, use another color to underline needed information.

   2. How many copies of *Astro Rider* were sold from July through November?

   Step 1: Read the problem.

   What information do you need to solve the problem?

   the _____ sold for each of the 5 months

   Step 2: Reread the article, underlining the needed information.

   How many copies were sold?

   _____, _____, _____, _____, _____

   Step 3: Add to solve the problem.

   _____ + _____ + _____ + _____

   + _____ = _____

   So, _____ copies were sold from July through November.

Name _____

PRACTICE

Use this article to find the needed information to solve problems 3–6.

Seeing Things in a Different Light

You can tell it's winter—it's already dark when you get home from work. And the welcoming porch light has burned out again. It seems you changed that hard-to-reach lightbulb just last week. Lightbulbs don't last very long. However, scientists have recently come up with a bright idea.

The E-bulb is a new lightbulb that works by making radio waves! Yes, it's a mystery to me, too, but it really works. Scientists say that an E-bulb should last for about 14 years. A regular bulb usually lasts less than a single year. E-bulbs will also use much less electricity. A regular bulb lit for 24 hours a day costs about $1.50 a week to power. An E-bulb would cost only about $0.45. Less electricity means less burning of fossil fuels and less pollution from power plants, as well as less to pay when the electric bill arrives.

So what's the drawback? Well, an E-bulb will probably sell for about $15—that's 20 times as much as a regular bulb. But because of its long life and low running costs, it will still save you money as it welcomes you home on those dark winter nights.

---

3. What information do you need to find out how much it would cost to light an E-bulb all the time for 52 weeks—a whole year? How much would it cost?

_____
_____
_____

4. What information in the news article can you use to find out how much a regular lightbulb sells for? How much does a regular bulb sell for?

_____
_____
_____

Solve . . . .

5. About how much does it cost to keep a regular bulb lit all day?

_____

6. How much longer than a regular bulb should an E-bulb last?

_____

● Multiplying and Dividing with Money

TEST-TAKING PRACTICE
Use this article to help you choose the best answer for each problem.

> ### A Walk in the Park
> They have been walking for 4 days now and have covered 50 miles of trails through Canyonlands National Park in Utah. Most of the group of hikers have blisters, and a few have sunburned faces and arms. But nobody is ready to call it a day. As one hiker says, "Joe wouldn't quit, and neither will I."
>
> She's referring to Joe Hendrix, a retired schoolteacher from Arizona, who founded "A Walk in the Park" in 1994. In the years since, a total of 625 people—students, professionals, and even a handful of celebrities—have taken time from their busy schedules to walk the trails of America's national parks. Each hiker pays $55 for the privilege of roughing it for a week. It's another $80 for the specialized equipment that the hiker will use. Food for the outing costs $65. (Clean socks are each hiker's own responsibility.) Groups of volunteers travel through the national parks, making measurements, taking readings, and comparing data. The information that they gather is used by Joe's organization in its studies of the environment.

1. **Which equation shows the amount each hiker pays?**

   A $80 + $65 = $145
   B $55 + $80 + $65 = $200
   C $55 + $80 = $135
   D Not given

2. **Which information would you use to find the average distance the hikers covered each day?**

   J Each hiker pays $55 for the privilege of roughing it for a week.
   K A total of 625 people have taken time.
   L They have walked for 4 days and have covered 50 miles.
   M Joe Hendrix founded "A Walk in the Park" in 1994.

3. **If each group includes 25 people, how many groups have taken "A Walk in the Park?"**

   A 25   C 625
   B 50   M 1994

Write About It
Write a plan, and then solve.

4. **If the group plans to hike 84 miles, how would you find how many more miles they must travel?**

   _____

   _____

   _____

   _____

1. A☐ B☐ C☐ D☐
2. J☐ K☐ L☐ M☐
3. A☐ B☐ C☐ D☐

● Multiplying and Dividing with Money

Reading a Circle Graph

Sometimes, you will find the information you need to solve a problem in a circle graph. A circle graph compares the parts of a whole.

The youth club held a walk-a-thon to raise funds for the youth center. The graph shows how the raised funds were used.

A. The title of the circle graph describes what the whole circle represents. The sectors of the circle show the parts that make up the whole. The size of each sector shows you how large a portion of the whole it represents.

B. You can compare two sectors by comparing their central angles.

Example 1

Did the club use more of the funds for building improvements or for new plumbing for the youth center?

> **Step 1:** Find the sectors labeled "building improvements" and "new plumbing."
>
> **Step 2:** Compare the size of the two sectors. **Which of the two sectors is larger?**
>
> Angle 1 is greater than 90°, and angle 2 is 90°.
>
> The sector labeled _____ is larger.
>
> **So, the club used more funds for _____.**

C. You can use the size of the central angle to estimate the fraction of the whole that a sector shows.

Example 2

About what fraction of the funds raised was used for new electrical wiring for the youth center?

> **Step 1:** Find the sector labeled "new electrical wiring."
>
> **Step 2:** Compare the size of the two sectors.
>
> **About how much of the circle is taken up by that sector? _____**
>
> **So, about _____ of the funds was used for new wiring.**

● Comparing and Ordering

GUIDED PRACTICE

Use the circle graph of the youth club's funds to find the
information you need to solve the problems.

Notice that the title of the graph now tells
you that the whole circle represents $1,000.

Funds Raised by the
Youth Club – $1,000

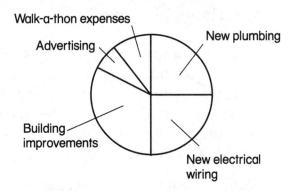

1. About how much did the club spend
   for new plumbing?

   a. Find the sector labeled
   "new plumbing."

   Estimate what fraction of the circle it
   represents.

   **About how much of the circle is taken
   up by the plumbing sector?**

   _____

   b. Multiply the whole amount, $1,000, by the fraction.

   $1000 x _____ = $ _____

   So, the club spent about _____ on new plumbing.

2. Which project did the club spend about $300 on?

   a. Find what fraction $300 is of $1,000. $300 ÷ 1,000 = _____

   b. Find that sector on the graph that is about $\frac{3}{10}$ of the whole.

   Which sector takes up about $\frac{3}{10}$ of the circle?

   (*Hint:* $\frac{3}{10}$ is greater than one fourth.)

   The sector labeled _____ takes up about $\frac{3}{10}$ of the circle.

   So, the club spent about $300 on _____.

3. Did the club spend more on plumbing or on advertising and expenses?

   a. Find the sectors with the corresponding labels.
   Compare the size of the plumbing sector with the *combined*
   size of the advertising and expenses sectors.

   Which takes up more of the circle? _____

   b. So, the club spent more on _____.

PRACTICE

Use the circle graph to find the information you need to solve the problems.

4. **What are the three most common elements in the earth's crust?**

The circle graph shows the elements in the earth's crust.

_____

5. **What is the most common element in the earth's crust?**

_____

6. **About how much of the earth's crust is made up of silicon?**

_____

Elements in the Earth's Crust

Solve . . . .

To solve these problems, you might find it helpful to mark or draw on the graph.

7. **Does oxygen make up more than half of the earth's crust or less than half of the earth's crust?**

_____

8. **Do aluminum and silicon together make up more or less of the earth's crust than oxygen?**

_____

9. **About how many tons of silicon would there be in a representative sample of 10 tons of the earth's crust?**

_____

10. **Which element would make up nearly 1 ton of a representative sample of 10 tons of the earth's crust?**

_____

● Comparing and Ordering

Use the graph to choose the best answer for problems 1–6. In the answer section at the bottom of the page, fill in the box of your choice.

A Collection of 80
Animal Trading Cards

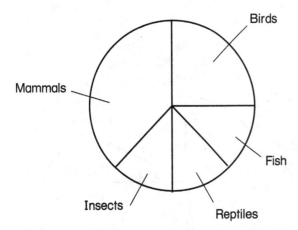

1. **Which of the following cards make up the same fraction of the total amount of cards as the mammal trading cards?**

    A fish and reptile cards together
    B insect and reptile cards together
    C fish and insect cards together
    D bird and fish cards together

2. **About what fraction of the collection do fish cards account for?**

    J $\frac{1}{10}$ L $\frac{1}{6}$

    K $\frac{1}{8}$ M $\frac{1}{4}$

3. **Which cards account for one-fourth of the collection?**

    A Birds   C Insects
    B Fish   D Mammals

4. **How would you compare reptile and insect cards?**

    J There are more insect cards.
    K There are more reptile cards.
    L There are the same number of each.
    M There are twice as many insect cards.

5. **About how many bird cards are there in the collection?**

    A 10   C 30
    B 20   D 40

6. **Which group has at least 10 cards?**

    J Fish   L Every group
    K Reptiles   M Not given

Write About It

7. **Why is a circle graph a useful way of showing how the parts of a whole compare?**

    _____

    _____

    _____

1. A ☐ B ☐ C ☐ D ☐   4. J ☐ K ☐ L ☐ M ☐

2. J ☐ K ☐ L ☐ M ☐   5. A ☐ B ☐ C ☐ D ☐

3. A ☐ B ☐ C ☐ D ☐   6. J ☐ K ☐ L ☐ M ☐

● Comparing and Ordering

Reading a Double-Bar Graph

A double-bar graph compares related sets of information. The graph below compares the numbers of viewers of the season premieres in 1998 and 1999 for four television shows.

Example

How many more viewers did *The Thompsons* have in 1999 than in 1998?

A. Find the double bar that is labeled *The Thompsons*.

B. The **key** next to the graph tells you what each bar represents.

   The black bar shows the number of viewers in 1998.

   The red bar shows the number of viewers in

   _____.

C. Find the value of each interval on the vertical axis.

   Count the number of intervals between 0 and 5 million.

   There are _____ intervals.

   So, each interval represents _____ viewers.

D. Now find the number of viewers of *The Thompsons* in each year. If the value lies between grid lines, estimate the amount.

   The Thompsons had _____ viewers in 1998.

   The Thompsons had _____ viewers in 1999.

E. Subtract to solve.

   9.5 – _____ = _____

   So, *The Thompsons* had _____ more viewers in 1999 than in 1998.

● Comparing and Ordering

GUIDED PRACTICE

Use the double-bar graph to answer the questions.

1. Which of the three movies had the lowest ticket sales on Saturday?

   Step 1: Find the bars that represent Saturday ticket sales.

   Which color bars represent Saturday ticket sales?

   the _____ bars

   Step 2: Compare the heights of the Saturday bars.

   Which Saturday bar is the shortest?

   The bar for _____ is the shortest.

   So, *Bandits* had the lowest ticket sales on Saturday.

2. Which movie had ticket sales of 650 tickets? On which day?

   Step 1: Find the value of each interval on the vertical axis.

   How many intervals are there between 0 and 800? _____

   Divide 800 by the number of intervals. 800 ÷ _____ = _____

   So, each interval represents 200 tickets sold.

   Step 2: Find the bar that corresponds to a value of about 650 on the vertical axis.

   THINK: The value 650 will be between 600 and 800, but it will be closer to 600.

   Which bar corresponds to about 650?

   the _____ bar for the movie _____

   So, _____ had ticket sales of about 650 on _____.

PRACTICE

Use the double-bar graph to answer the questions.

3. **Which vendor sold the most hot dogs?**

_____

4. **Which vendor sold the most pretzels?**

_____

5. **Which vendor sold 30 pretzels?**

_____

Solve . . . .

6. **How many more hot dogs did Harrison sell than Paul sold?**

_____

7. **How many more hot dogs than pretzels did Harrison sell?**

_____

8. **How many hot dogs and pretzels did Paul sell all together?**

_____

9. **Which of the three vendors sold 10 more pretzels than hot dogs?**

_____

10. **Hot dogs and pretzels each sell for the same amount. Which of the three vendors took in the most money from sales?**

_____

11. **If hot dogs and pretzels sell for the same amount, did the vendors take in more money from selling hot dogs or from selling pretzels?**

_____

● Comparing and Ordering

TEST-TAKING PRACTICE

Use the double-bar graph to answer the questions. Choose the best answer for each problem. In the answer section at the bottom of the page, fill in the box of your choice.

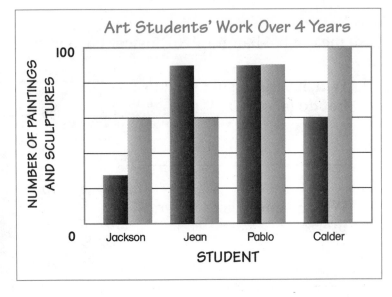

Art Students' Work Over 4 Years

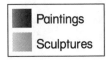

Paintings

Sculptures

1. **Which statement is false?**

   A The black bars show the number of paintings done.
   B Jackson and Jean made the same number of sculptures.
   C Pablo made the same number of paintings and sculptures.
   D Calder made the most paintings.

2. **Which statement is true?**

   J The gray bars show the number of paintings done.
   K Pablo made the same number of paintings as Jean.
   L Calder made the most paintings.
   M Jackson made 60 paintings.

3. **Which art student made the most sculptures?**

   A Jackson   C Pablo
   B Jean   D Calder

4. **How many paintings did the four students make combined?**

   J 100   L 270
   K 250   M 310

5. **How many works did Jackson make in all?**

   A 90   C 60
   B 150   D 30

Write About It

6. **If each student also made a number of photographs, how could you show the data in the graph?**

   _____

   _____

   _____

1. A ☐ B ☐ C ☐ D ☐   4. J ☐ K ☐ L ☐ M ☐

2. J ☐ K ☐ L ☐ M ☐   5. A ☐ B ☐ C ☐ D ☐

3. A ☐ B ☐ C ☐ D ☐

● Comparing and Ordering

Test-Taking Skill: Eliminating Choices

On a multiple choice test, it's sometimes hard to find the right answer to a problem. It can help to eliminate choices that are wrong.

Example

Karen is ordering buttons for the bike club. The buttons cost $0.13 each if she buys 100 and $0.11 each if she buys more than 300. She decides to buy 750 buttons. How much will she pay?

A	$11.00	**C**	$97.50
B	$82.50	**D**	300

Step 1: Read the problem carefully. Think about the kind of answer you need. The answer to "How much will she pay?" is an amount of money. So, choice **D** must be wrong.

Step 2: Karen will pay $0.11 per button because she is buying more than 300 buttons. Estimate to eliminate choices.

THINK: The price of $0.11 is close to $0.10, and 750 x $0.10 is $75.00.

$0.11 is more than $0.10, which tells you that the answer has to be more than $75.00. So, choice **A**, $11.00, is too small.

You can eliminate choice **A**.

The choices left are choice **B**, $82.50, and choice **C**, $97.50.

Both are greater than $75.00.

Divide or multiply to find the correct answer:

B $\rightarrow$ $82.50 ÷ 0.11 = _____   750 x $0.11= _____

Karen will pay _____ for 750 buttons.

So, the correct answer is _____.

© 1999 Metropolitan Teaching & Learning Co.

Choose the best answer for each problem. In the answer section at the bottom of this page, fill in the box of your choice. For problem 1, explain how you found the answer.

1. The marching band sold T-shirts for $7.50 each. They sold 36 T-shirts at the game.

   How much money did they earn?

   A 270 T-shirts   C $270.00
   B $27.00   D $2,700

   _____

   _____

   _____

   _____

   _____

   _____

   _____

2. The sign at the Super Cinema has 15 rows of lightbulbs. Each row has 220 bulbs.

   How many bulbs are there in all?

   J 220 bulbs   L 330 bulbs
   K 220 rows   M 3,300 bulbs

3. A jet airplane flies at about 580 miles per hour.

   About how many miles can it travel in 4 hours?

   A About 200 miles per hour
   B About 2,400 miles
   C About 5,800 miles
   D About 7,400 miles

4. A housefly lays 120 eggs. Half of the eggs hatch and become female flies.

   If each of those females lays 120 eggs, how many flies would hatch in the next generation?

   J 60 eggs   L 720 flies
   K 120 flies   M 7,200 flies

5. The speed at which Pluto orbits the sun is 2.9 miles per second. Mercury orbits the sun 10 times as fast as Pluto.

   How fast does Mercury move?

   A 10 miles per second
   B 29 miles an hour
   C 29 miles per second
   D 290 miles per second

1. A ☐ B ☐ C ☐ D ☐
2. J ☐ K ☐ L ☐ M ☐
3. A ☐ B ☐ C ☐ D ☐
4. J ☐ K ☐ L ☐ M ☐

5. A ☐ B ☐ C ☐ D ☐

● Test-Taking Skill

Name _____

Using a Table to Rename Measures

To solve some measurement problems, you'll have to rename a measure with a different unit. If you don't already know the equivalent measures, you can find the needed information in a table like the one below.

Metric Units of Measure

Units of Length	Units of Capacity	Units of Mass
1 meter (m) = 1,000 millimeters (mm)	1 kiloliter (kL) = 1,000 liters (L)	1 gram (g) = 1,000 milligrams (mg)
1 meter (m) = 100 centimeters (cm)	1 liter = 1,000 milliliters (mL)	1 kilogram (kg) = 1,000 grams (g)
1 kilometer (km) = 1,000 meters		

Example

There is a 2-kg bag of iron filings and a 200-g bag of calcium carbonate in the cupboard. Drew's science teacher asks him to bring the heavier bag. Which bag should Drew bring?

A. Look at the problem carefully.

What measurements do you need to compare?

_____

B. Look at the table. Find the column that shows grams and kilograms. Underline the equation that you need to use.

Write an equation to show how the units compare.

1 kg = _____ g

C. Rename the larger unit so that you can compare the measures. Multiply to get the measure that you need (2 kilograms).

2 kg = 2 x _____ g   2 kg = 2,000 g

D. Now compare the two sizes of bags.

2,000 g > 200 g

2 kg is greater than 200 g.

So, Drew should bring the _____ bag.

● Multiplication Facts

GUIDED PRACTICE

Metric Units of Measure

Units of Length	Units of Capacity	Units of Mass
1 meter (m) = 1,000 millimeters (mm)	1 kiloliter (kL) = 1,000 liters (L)	1 gram (g) = 1,000 milligrams (mg)
1 meter = 100 centimeters (cm)	1 liter = 1,000 milliliters (mL)	1 kilogram (kg) = 1,000 grams
1 kilometer (km) = 1,000 meters		

1. Two bottles are filled with water. One bottle holds 750 mL and the other holds 0.6 L. Which bottle is smaller?

   a. What measurements do you need to compare? _____

   b. Find the appropriate column of the table.
      Write an equation for comparing the units.

   1 L = _____

   c. **Rename the larger measure by multiplying.**

   0.6 L = _____ x 1,000 mL = _____ mL

   d. **Compare the capacities of the bottles.**

   _____ < _____

   So, the bottle holding _____ is the smaller bottle.

2. Rolls of fabric come in two different widths: 120 cm and 1.75 m. Which is the wider roll?

   a. **What measurements do you need to compare?** _____

   b. Find the appropriate column of the table.
      Write an equation for comparing the units.

   1 m = _____ cm

   c. **Rename the larger measure by multiplying.**

   1.75 m = _____ x 100 cm

   d. **Compare the widths of the rolls.**

   _____ cm > _____ cm

   So, the roll that is _____ wide is the wider roll.

PRACTICE

Solve each problem by renaming one of the measures. If you wish, use the table below to find equivalent measures.

Metric Units of Measure

Units of Length	Units of Capacity	Units of Mass
1 meter (m) = 1,000 millimeters (mm)	1 kiloliter (kL) = 1,000 liters (L)	1 gram (g) = 1,000 milligrams (mg)
1 meter = 100 centimeters (cm)	1 liter = 1,000 milliliters (mL)	1 kilogram (kg) = 1,000 grams
1 kilometer (km) = 1,000 meters		

3. The minimum requirement for a vitamin is 4 mg. A serving of cereal has 0.0033 g of the vitamin. **Would one serving be enough?**

_____

_____

4. Karin is mailing two packages. One has a mass of 3,500 g. The other has a mass of 1.8 kg. **Which package has the greater mass?**

_____

_____

5. Torkil runs 16 kilometers per week. Chris runs 10,000 meters per week? **Who runs farther?**

_____

_____

6. A model car is 0.15 meter long and a model bus is 110 millimeters long. **Which model is longer?**

_____

_____

7. A 3-kg weight is on the left side of a balance scale. A 4,000-g weight is on the right side. **Which side is heavier?**

_____

8. Katy can jump 120 cm high on Earth and 7 m high on the moon. **Which jump is higher?**

_____

9. One drinking glass holds 450 mL while another holds 0.5 L. **Which glass holds more?**

_____

10. A jar holds 1,850 mL of water. **If the water is poured into a 2-L saucepan, will the saucepan overflow?**

_____

For problems 1–3, choose the best way to rename units for the problem. For problems 4 and 5, choose the best answer to fill in the blank. Use the table on page 87 if you need help with equivalents. In the answer section at the bottom of the page, fill in the box of your choice.

1. Jill is 154 cm tall, and Jim is 1.3 m tall. Who is taller?

    A $1.3 \times 1,000 = 1,300$ mm
    B $1.3 \times 100 = 130$ cm
    C $54 \div 10 = 5.4$ m
    D $0.3 \times 1,000 = 300$ mm

2. A beaker contains 1,500 mL of water. If the water is poured into a 2-L bowl, will it overflow?

    J $1,500 \div 2 = 750$ mL
    K $1,500 \div 100 = 15$ L
    L $2 \times 100 = 200$ mL
    M $2 \times 1,000 = 2,000$ mL

3. A geologist discovered a fossil with a mass of 3.4 kg and another fossil with a mass of 1,670 g. Which fossil has the greater mass?

    A $1,670 \times 1,000 = 1,670,000$ mg
    B $3.4 \times 100 = 340$ g
    C $3.4 \times 1,000 = 3,400$ g
    D $1,670 \div 100 = 16.7$ kg

4. A 0.4-km race is _____ a 400-m race.

    J the same length as
    K shorter than
    L longer than
    M twice as long as

5. A 2.2-kg box of nails has _____ a box of nails with a mass of 275 g.

    A the same mass as
    B almost the same mass as
    C less mass than
    D greater mass than

Write About It

6. Which is the more reasonable estimate for the capacity of a bathtub: 20 L or 20 kL?

    Write a plan for solving the problem. Then solve.

    _____

    _____

    _____

    _____

1. A ☐ B ☐ C ☐ D ☐   4. J ☐ K ☐ L ☐ M ☐

2. J ☐ K ☐ L ☐ M ☐   5. A ☐ B ☐ C ☐ D ☐

3. A ☐ B ☐ C ☐ D ☐

● Multiplication Facts

Deciding How to Rename Customary Measures

When a problem has different units, you'll need to show the information in another way to solve the problem. When you rename measures, you multiply or divide. Drawing a picture can help you decide which to do.

Customary Units of Measure

Units of Length	Units of Capacity	Units of Mass
1 foot (ft) = 12 inches (in.)	1 cup (c) = 8 fluid ounces (fl oz)	1 pound (lb) = 16 ounces (oz)
1 yard (yd) = 3 feet	1 quart (qt) = 4 cups	1 ton (T) = 2,000 pounds
1 mile (mi) = 5,280 feet	1 gallon (gal) = 4 quarts	

Example

A roll of carpet is 11 yards 2 feet long. Is it long enough to carpet a hallway that is 32 feet long?

A. Look at the problem carefully.

What measurements do you need to compare?

_____

B. Rename so that both measurements use the same units. If you aren't sure whether to multiply or divide, draw a picture of the units.

_____ = ____ ____ ____
yd   ft   ft   ft

THINK: Yards are larger than feet. So, **multiply** to rename yards as feet. **Divide** to rename feet as yards.

Rename the measurement that has mixed units.

11 yd = 11 x _____ ft → 33 ft

So, 11 yd 2 ft = 33 ft + 2 ft → 35 ft

C. Compare the measurements to solve the problem.

35 ft > 32 ft

So, the roll of carpet is long enough.

Customary Units of Measure

Units of Length	Units of Capacity	Units of Mass
1 foot (ft) = 12 inches (in.)	1 cup (c) = 8 fluid ounces (fl oz)	1 pound (lb) = 16 ounces (oz)
1 yard (yd) = 3 feet	1 quart (qt) = 4 cups	1 ton (T) = 2,000 pounds
1 mile (mi) = 5,280 feet	1 gallon (gal) = 4 quarts	

1. A truck can carry a load of 5 tons. Is it safe to load 8,000 lb of rock onto the truck?

   a. What measurements do you need to compare? _____

   b. Rename so that both measurements use the same units.

   THINK: When you rename a measurement in larger units, there will be fewer of them. You should **divide**.

    1 lb   1 ton

   Rename one measurement.

   8,000 ÷ _____ = 4

   c. Compare the measurements.

   _____ < _____

   So, it _____ safe to load 8,000 lb onto the truck.

2. Sarah needs to buy 9 gallons of oil. It comes in 1-quart cans. How many cans should she buy?

   a. What measurements do you need to compare?

   _____

   b. Rename so that both measurements use the same units.

   THINK: When you rename a measurement in smaller units, there will be more of them. You should **multiply**.

   Rename one measurement. Then compare measurements.

   9 x _____ = 36   _____ gal = _____ qt

   So, Sarah should buy _____ cans of oil.

© 1999 Metropolitan Teaching & Learning Co.

PRACTICE

Solve. Show your work. Use the table to help you change units of measurement.

Customary Units of Measurement

Units of Length	Units of Capacity	Units of Mass
1 foot (ft) = 12 inches (in.)	1 cup (c) = 8 fluid ounces (fl oz)	1 pound (lb) = 16 ounces (oz)
1 yard (yd) = 3 feet	1 quart (qt) = 4 cups	1 ton (T) = 2,000 pounds
1 mile (mi) = 5,280 feet	1 gallon (gal) = 4 quarts	

3. A serving of juice is 1 cup. **How many servings are there in 6 quarts of juice?**

_____

_____

4. A dose of cold medicine is 2 fl oz. **How many doses does a 2-cup bottle hold?**

_____

_____

5. A 2-ton load of bricks is delivered. The next morning, it weighs 3,800 lb. **Have bricks been added to or removed from the load?**

_____

_____

_____

6. A gas tank can hold 9 gallons. **If there are 19 quarts of gas in the tank, is it more or less than half full?**

_____

_____

7. Two boxes of rice are the same price. One contains 40 oz rice, and the other contains 2 lb 2 oz rice. **Which box is the better buy?**

_____

_____

8. A meteor's speed is measured at 10,000 feet per second. Later, its speed is 2 miles per second. **Has the meteor sped up or slowed down?**

_____

_____

For questions 1–3, choose the best way to rename units for each problem. For questions 4 and 5, choose the best answer for each problem. Fill in the box of your choice in the answer section at the bottom of this page.

1. **A fish tank is 26 in. long and 2 ft high. Is the tank longer than it is high?**

   A $12 \div 2 = 6$ ft
   B $26 - 12 = 14$ in.
   C $26 \div 2 = 13$ in.
   D $2 \times 12 = 24$ in.

2. **A horse weighs 2,500 lb. Can it be carried in a truck that has a 2-ton weight limit?**

   J $2 \times 2,500 = 5,000$ lb
   K $2,500 \div 2 = 1,250$ lb
   L $2 \times 2,000 = 4,000$ lb
   M $2,500 - 2,000 = 500$ lb

3. **Sarah is pouring 1-cup servings from 3 gallons of fruit punch. How many servings can she pour?**

   A $3 \times 4 \times 4 = 48$ cups
   B $3 \times 4 = 12$ cups
   C $3 + 3 + 3 = 9$ cups
   D $4 \times 4 \times 4 = 64$ cups

4. **How many 2-ft lengths of wood can be cut from a 4-yd plank?**

   J 6   L 8
   K 12   M 10

5. **Jerry adds 2 gal orange juice, 3 qt pineapple juice, and 1 qt soda water to make a fruit punch. How much punch does he make?**

   A 4 gal   C $2\frac{1}{2}$ gal
   B 3 gal   D 3 gal 2 qt

Write About It

Write a plan for solving the following problem. Then solve.

6. **Debra is making fruit punch to sell by the cup. How many cups of punch can she sell if she makes 10 qt?**

   _____

   _____

   _____

   _____

---

1. A ☐ B ☐ C ☐ D ☐   4. J ☐ K ☐ L ☐ M ☐

2. J ☐ K ☐ L ☐ M ☐   5. A ☐ B ☐ C ☐ D ☐

3. A ☐ B ☐ C ☐ D ☐

● Multiplication and Divisions

Deciding How to Show Measures Another Way

You often have to add, subtract, multiply, or divide in measurement problems. You may first need to decide how to show the measurements in a way that makes computing easier.

Example

A maple tree was 3 ft 5 in. tall when it was planted. The tree has now reached a height of 6 ft 3 in. How much has the tree grown?

3 ft 5 in.   6 ft 3 in.

A. Make a drawing to picture the problem. You can see from the drawing that you need to subtract.

Decide how to solve the problem.

Subtract _____ from _____.

B. **Rename the measurements as just one unit.**

6 ft → 6 x _____ in. → 72 in.

So, 6 ft 3 in. → 72 + 3 → _____

3 ft → _____ x 12 in. → 36 in.

So, 3 ft 5 in. → 36 + 5 → _____

On your diagram, write in the renamed measures.

C. **Calculate the answer.** 75 – _____ = _____ in.

So, the tree has grown _____ in.

1. A recipe calls for 2 ounces of peanuts per serving. How many servings can Dana make from a 3-pound bag of peanuts?

   a. Make a drawing to picture the problem. Label the measures.

      Decide how to solve the problem.

      Divide _____ lb by 2 oz.

   b. **Rename the pounds as ounces.**

      3 lb → 3 x 16 oz → _____ oz

   3 lb   2 oz

   On your diagram, cross out the pound measure, and write in the renamed measure.

   c. **Calculate the answer.**

      48 oz ÷ 2 oz = _____

   So, Dana can make _____ servings.

2. An empty water tank can hold 6 gallons. If each of 10 people carries a 3-qt bucket of water from a lake, can they fill the tank?

   a. **Decide how to solve the problem.**

      Multiply _____ qt by 10.

   b. **Perform the computation.**

      3 qt x 10 = _____ qt

   c. **Rename the quarts as gallons.**

      30 qt → 30 ÷ 4 → 7.5 gal

   d. **Compare the measurements.**

      7.5 gal > 6 gal

   So, they _____ fill the tank.

PRACTICE

Solve. Show your work. Use the table to help you rename units of measure.

Customary Units of Measure

Units of Length	Units of Capacity	Units of Mass
1 foot (ft) = 12 inches (in.)	1 cup (c) = 8 fluid ounces (fl oz)	1 pound (lb) = 16 ounces (oz)
1 yard (yd) = 3 feet	1 quart (qt) = 4 cups	1 ton (T) = 2,000 pounds
1 mile (mi) = 5,280 feet	1 gallon (gal) = 4 quarts	

3. A carpenter uses a 5 ft 4 in. length of wood for the four legs of a coffee table. How long is each leg?

_____

_____

4. Donnel is 3 in. less than 6 ft tall. How tall is he?

_____

_____

5. A truck weighs 3,000 lb. It is filled with 2,500 lb of gravel. Can the truck safely cross a bridge with a weight limit of 4 T?

_____

_____

_____

6. A jeweler has 1 lb 4 oz of silver to use for 5 bracelets. If each bracelet is the same, how much silver will each bracelet have?

_____

_____

7. Joe's summer tour lasts 3 weeks and 5 days. He has been touring for 1 week and 6 days. For how many more days will Joe be on tour?

_____

_____

8. A chef is feeding 200 people. If she expects each person to drink 2 cups of soda, how many gallons of soda should the chef buy?

_____

_____

● Multiplying and Dividing

Choose the best answer for each problem. In the answer section
at the bottom of the page, fill in the box of your choice.

1. **Four babies have the weights shown. Which baby weighs the most?**

   A 288 oz   **C** 19 lb
   B 18 lb 2 oz   **D** 300 oz

2. **At a track meet, Bjorn's first jump measured 3 yd 1 ft 5 in. His second jump measured 3 yd 2 ft 3 in. How much longer was his second jump than his first?**

   J 10 in.   **L** 2 ft 2 in.
   K 1 ft 10 in.   **M** 4 ft 8 in.

3. **How many cakes can Kayla bake with 3 qt of milk if each cake requires 6 fl oz of milk?**

   A 10   **C** 25
   B 16   **D** 30

4. **A carpenter cuts a 2 ft 4 in. length off a plank that measured 2 yd 1 ft. How long is the plank now?**

   J 4 ft 8 in.   **L** 3 yd 4 in.
   K 2 ft 4 in.   **M** 8 in.

5. **Darshana weighs 109 lb 7 oz, and her kitten weighs 3 lb 10 oz. If she stands on a scale, holding her kitten, what will the scale read?**

   A 105 lb 1 oz
   B 105 lb 13 oz
   C 112 lb 1 oz
   D 113 lb 1 oz

Write About It

Write a plan for solving the following problem. Then solve.

6. **An elevator can carry a maximum weight of 1 T. Twelve people are waiting for the elevator. If each person weighs about 180 lb, can they all ride the elevator safely?**

   _____

   _____

   _____

   _____

   _____

   _____

1. A ☐ B ☐ C ☐ D ☐   4. J ☐ K ☐ L ☐ M ☐
2. J ☐ K ☐ L ☐ M ☐   5. A ☐ B ☐ C ☐ D ☐
3. A ☐ B ☐ C ☐ D ☐

Using Benchmarks

When you have to solve problems with fractions, look first at the denominators. If the fractions have the same denominators, you can simply compare the numerators. Otherwise, you may find it easiest to use number sense.

If the fractions in a problem have different denominators, think about how close each fraction is to 0, $\frac{1}{2}$, or 1.

- If the numerator is a small number and the denominator is a large number, the fraction is close to 0—for example: $\frac{1}{8}$, $\frac{4}{25}$, $\frac{11}{100}$.

- If the numerator is about half the denominator, the fraction is close to $\frac{1}{2}$—for example: $\frac{5}{8}$, $\frac{13}{25}$, $\frac{58}{100}$.

- If the numerator and denominator are about the same, the fraction is close to 1—for example: $\frac{7}{8}$, $\frac{23}{25}$, $\frac{97}{100}$.

Example

Mrs. Wong wants the widest wallpaper border. Which of the three borders is the widest?

Border	Width
solid	$2\frac{5}{8}$ in.
geometric	$2\frac{13}{16}$ in.
flowered	$2\frac{1}{4}$ in.

A. First, compare the whole-number parts of the three mixed numbers. **Is there any difference among the whole-number parts of the fractions?**

_____

B. If the whole-number parts are the same, compare the fraction parts.

THINK: 5 is about half of 8. So, $\frac{5}{8}$ is close to _____.

13 and 16 are about the same. So, $\frac{13}{16}$ is close to _____.

1 is much smaller than 4. So, $\frac{1}{4}$ is close to _____.

C. Now use your approximations with the mixed numbers.

$2\frac{5}{8}$ is close to _____.

$2\frac{13}{16}$ is close to _____.

$2\frac{1}{4}$ is close to _____.

D. Compare the approximations.

Which mixed number is greatest? _____

So, the _____ border is the widest.

• Comparing and Ordering Fractions

GUIDED PRACTICE

1. Jenny and Troy see this sign at the Visitor's Center of an amusement park. Which is closer to the Visitor's Center, Dinosaur Village or the Water Slide?

Visitor's Center
Dinosaur Village... $\frac{3}{8}$ mi ⟶
⟵ Water Slide... $\frac{9}{10}$ mi

Step 1: **Write down the distances you will compare.**

Dinosaur Village is _____ mi from the Visitor's Center.

The Water Slide is _____ mi from the Visitor's Center.

Step 2: Use benchmarks to compare the fractions.

Is $\frac{3}{8}$ closest to 0, $\frac{1}{2}$, or 1? _____

Is $\frac{9}{10}$ closest to 0, $\frac{1}{2}$, or 1? _____

Step 3: **Compare the approximations from Step 2.**

$\frac{1}{2} < 1$. So, _____ < _____.

So, _____ is closer to the visitor's center.

2. Fred wants to hike on the longest trail. He reads the sign at the right. Which trail should he take?

Red Trail	$4\frac{5}{8}$ mi
Yellow Trail	$4\frac{1}{2}$ mi
Blue Trail	$5\frac{1}{8}$ mi

Step 1: **Write down the distances you will compare.**

Red Trail is _____ mi long.

Yellow Trail is _____ mi long.

Blue Trail is _____ mi long.

Step 2: Compare the mixed numbers.

Which whole number is greatest? _____

Step 3: If one of the whole-number parts is greatest, that mixed number is the greatest. You don't have to compare the fractions.

Which trail is longest? the _____ Trail

So, Fred should take the _____ Trail.

© 1999 Metropolitan Teaching & Learning Co.

98

Name _____

PRACTICE

Solve. Use benchmark fractions to help you.

3. A store is displaying three bookshelves in order from least to greatest height. The heights of the bookshelves are $4\frac{1}{6}$ ft, $4\frac{7}{8}$ ft, and $4\frac{5}{12}$ ft. In which order will the store display the shelves?

_____

4. Linda wants to bake a pie. The recipe calls for about $1\frac{1}{2}$ lb of cherries. At the grocery store, there are bags of cherries weighing $1\frac{7}{16}$ lb, $1\frac{7}{8}$ lb, and 2 lb. Which of the three bags should Linda buy?

_____

5. Three bags of grass seed at the store all sell for the same price. The bags weigh $7\frac{1}{4}$ lb, $7\frac{5}{8}$ lb, and $6\frac{7}{8}$ lb. Which of the bags is the best buy?

_____

6. Shelly has rolled-up ribbons labeled with these lengths: $3\frac{7}{8}$ ft, $3\frac{1}{4}$ ft, and $3\frac{7}{12}$ ft. If she wants to use the longest ribbon to hem a skirt, which ribbon should she use?

_____

7. Jake needs a rod to fit tightly into a hole with a diameter of 2 in. The hardware store has rods with the following diameters: $2\frac{1}{8}$ in., $1\frac{1}{4}$ in., $1\frac{3}{16}$ in., $1\frac{7}{8}$ in., and $1\frac{7}{16}$ in. Which rod will fit the hole most tightly?

_____

8. Jorge is tired from hiking and wants to take the shortest route back to camp. The Willow Trail is $1\frac{3}{10}$-km long. The Forest Trail is $2\frac{1}{5}$-km long, and the Pond Trail is $1\frac{7}{8}$-km long. Which of the trails should he take back?

_____

9. A scientist has four drums of the same chemical. The drums hold $7\frac{3}{32}$ gallons, $7\frac{9}{16}$ gallons, $6\frac{31}{32}$ gallons, and $7\frac{7}{16}$ gallons. Which of the drums holds the most?

_____

10. Three athletes competed in a long-jump event. Stephen's jump measured $11\frac{7}{12}$ ft. Johanne's jump measured $12\frac{1}{4}$ ft, and Raiku's jump measured $11\frac{5}{6}$ ft. Which of the athletes won the event?

_____

© 1999 Metropolitan Teaching & Learning Co.

For problems 1–5, choose the best answer for each problem. In the answer section at the bottom of the page, fill in the box of your choice.

1. An electrician has lengths of wire measuring $3\frac{1}{8}$ ft, $2\frac{3}{4}$ ft, $3\frac{5}{8}$ ft, and $3\frac{11}{12}$ ft. **If he wants to use the longest piece, which should he pick?**

   A $3\frac{1}{8}$ ft   C $3\frac{5}{8}$ ft

   B $2\frac{3}{4}$ ft   D $3\frac{11}{12}$ ft

2. Donna needs about 2 lb of peanuts for a recipe. **Which of the following weights is closest to 2 lb?**

   J $2\frac{7}{16}$ lb   L $2\frac{1}{2}$ lb

   K $1\frac{7}{8}$ lb   M 3 lb

3. In the high jump, Pablo jumped 7 ft $5\frac{9}{16}$ in. Sam jumped 7 ft $4\frac{1}{12}$ in. Jeff jumped 7 ft $5\frac{11}{12}$ in. Alan jumped 7 ft $5\frac{7}{12}$ in. **Who jumped the highest?**

   A Pablo   C Jeff

   B Sam   D Alan

4. Why is the fraction $\frac{8}{15}$ close to $\frac{1}{2}$?

   J The numerator and the denominator are about the same.

   K The numerator is a small number.

   L The numerator is close to twice the denominator.

   M The numerator is close to half the denominator.

5. A dinosaur's leg bones can be clues to the size of the dinosaur. The longest bones usually come from the longest dinosaurs.

   Which one of the following leg bones probably came from the longest dinosaur?

   A Bone A: $6\frac{9}{10}$ ft

   B Bone B: $6\frac{1}{5}$ ft

   C Bone C: $6\frac{7}{10}$ ft

   D Bone D: $6\frac{1}{2}$ ft

Write About It

Write a plan for solving the following problem. Then solve.

6. **The three winning throws in a javelin-throwing contest were $75\frac{1}{8}$ yd, $74\frac{15}{16}$ yd, and $74\frac{3}{8}$ yd. Which throw earned second place?**

   _____

   _____

   _____

   _____

   _____

   _____

   _____

1. A☐ B☐ C☐ D☐   4. J☐ K☐ L☐ M☐

2. J☐ K☐ L☐ M☐   5. A☐ B☐ C☐ D☐

3. A☐ B☐ C☐ D☐

● Comparing and Ordering Fractions

Drawing a Number Line

To solve some problems, you'll have to add and subtract fractions. Drawing a number line to show the information can help you.

Example

The ceiling in Josh's room is 8 ft high. There is a shelf $5\frac{5}{6}$ ft above the floor. Can Josh place a painting that is $2\frac{1}{2}$ ft tall on the shelf?

A. Decide what you need to find out.

Is the sum of $5\frac{5}{6}$ and $2\frac{1}{2}$ less than _____?

B. Use benchmarks to approximate the larger number.

$\frac{5}{6}$ is close to 1. So, $5\frac{5}{6}$ is close to _____.

C. Draw a number line.

Mark the line with a dot a little to the left of 6.

D. Use benchmarks to approximate the smaller number.

$\frac{1}{2}$ is equal to $\frac{1}{2}$. So, use _____ as the smaller number.

E. Use the number line to count on from the dot.

Move $2\frac{1}{2}$ spaces to the right.

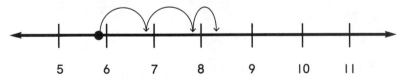

Does the point show less or more than 8? _____

So, Josh _____ place the painting on the shelf.

1. Dolores needs 5 lb of apples for a recipe. She split a bag of apples weighing $7\frac{5}{8}$ lb with Ralph, and gave him $2\frac{3}{16}$ lb of the apples. Does Dolores have enough apples left for her recipe?

   Step 1: Decide what you need to find out.

   Is the difference of $7\frac{5}{8}$ and $2\frac{3}{16}$ greater than _____?

   Step 2: Draw a number line.

   THINK: $7\frac{5}{8}$ is a little more than $7\frac{1}{2}$.

   Mark the line with a dot a little to the right of $7\frac{1}{2}$.

   Step 3: Use the number line to count down.

   THINK: $2\frac{3}{16}$ is a little more than 2.

   Move a little more than 2 spaces to the left.

   Does the point show less or more than 5?

   _____

   So, Dolores _____ enough apples.

2. A scientist mixes $3\frac{1}{3}$ pt of one liquid to $1\frac{1}{6}$ pt of another liquid. How many pints of the mixture does she have?

   Step 1: Decide what you need to find out.

   What is the sum of _____ and _____ ?

   Step 2: You need an exact answer.

   Can you use a number line? _____

   Write the numbers as equivalent fractions, and add.

   $$3\frac{2}{6} + 1\frac{1}{6} = 4\frac{3}{6}$$

   THINK: I can simplify $\frac{3}{6}$ to $\frac{1}{2}$.

   So, the scientist has _____ pt of the mixture.

   Check your answer on a number line. Mark a dot just to the left of $3\frac{1}{2}$. Move right a little more than 1 space.

PRACTICE

Mark on the number line to solve each problem.

Find the LCD to solve. Use a number line to check your answer.

3. Bill has two containers of water. One container has $5\frac{1}{8}$ pt, and the other has $2\frac{7}{12}$ pt. Can he pour both into an 8-pt bucket without its overflowing?

_____

4. A table is $3\frac{11}{12}$ ft wide, and a couch is $6\frac{2}{3}$ ft wide. Will they fit side by side along a wall that is 10 ft long?

_____

5. A jeweler has $9\frac{9}{16}$ oz of silver. He uses $4\frac{7}{8}$ oz for a bracelet. He wants to make a necklace that will take 5 oz of silver. Does he have enough left?

_____

6. A baby weighed $7\frac{1}{4}$ lb at birth. By the following January, the baby had gained $3\frac{1}{6}$ lb. How much did the baby weigh in January?

_____

7. An electrician uses a $4\frac{5}{8}$ ft length from a roll of $10\frac{11}{12}$ ft of wire. What length of wire does she have left?

_____

8. Two hiking trails measure $4\frac{3}{10}$ miles and $3\frac{1}{4}$ miles long. How many miles does Sven travel if he hikes both trails?

_____

● Adding and Subtracting Fractions

Choose the best answer for each problem. In the answer section
at the bottom of the page, fill in the box of your choice.

1. A tree was $5\frac{1}{6}$ ft tall two years
   ago. Since then, it has grown
   $4\frac{3}{8}$ ft taller. Which of the
   following statements is true?

   A The tree is less than 10 ft tall.
   B The tree is more than 10 ft tall.
   C The tree is exactly 10 ft tall.
   D The tree is exactly 9 ft tall.

2. Haruko took $1\frac{11}{12}$ lb of sugar from
   a bag that contained $4\frac{3}{8}$ lb of
   sugar. Which of the following
   statements is true?

   J The bag has less than 2 lb of
      sugar.
   K The bag has about $2\frac{1}{2}$ lb of
      sugar.
   L The bag has about 3 lb of
      sugar.
   M The bag has about $6\frac{1}{2}$ lb of
      sugar.

3. Sam pours $5\frac{3}{4}$ gallons of gas into
   a tank that already contains $1\frac{1}{8}$
   gallons. How much gas is in the
   tank?

   A $4\frac{5}{8}$ gal   C $6\frac{7}{8}$ gal
   B $6\frac{5}{8}$ gal   D 7 gal

4. A carpenter has a board that is
   $8\frac{2}{3}$ ft long. She cuts a $4\frac{1}{6}$ ft length
   off the board. How long is the
   remaining piece?

   J $4\frac{1}{2}$ ft   L 5 ft
   K $4\frac{5}{6}$ ft   M $12\frac{5}{6}$ ft

5. A child is now double her birth
   length. If she was $20\frac{1}{8}$ inches
   long at birth, how tall is she
   now?

   A $22\frac{1}{8}$ in.   C $40\frac{1}{4}$ in.
   B $40\frac{1}{8}$ in.   D $40\frac{1}{2}$ in.

Write About It

6. Explain how you can estimate
   answers to problems with
   fractions by using a number
   line.

   _____

   _____

   _____

   _____

   _____

   _____

1. A ☐ B ☐ C ☐ D ☐   4. J ☐ K ☐ L ☐ M ☐

2. J ☐ K ☐ L ☐ M ☐   5. A ☐ B ☐ C ☐ D ☐

3. A ☐ B ☐ C ☐ D ☐

● Adding and Subtracting Fractions

Test-Taking Skill: Writing a Plan

On some tests, you need to explain how to solve a problem. It is important to explain your thinking and to show your calculations.

Example

Kelly's television uses 0.20 kilowatt-hour of electricity every hour that it is on. She pays $0.12 for each kilowatt-hour. About how much does it cost to run her television for 4 hours?

A. Read the problem carefully. Decide on the kind of answer you need.

The answer is the amount of money it costs to run the television for 4 hours.

B. Write a plan for finding the answer.

1: First, I will find how much one hour of television costs by multiplying the number of kilowatt-hours by the cost per kilowatt-hour.

2: Then, I will multiply that product by 4 to find about how much 4 hours costs.

C. Follow your plan, and solve the problem. Show your calculations.

1:	$	0.12	Cost per kilowatt-hour
	x	0.20	Number of kilowatt-hours per hour of TV use
	$		Cost to run TV for one hour

2:	$		Cost to run TV for one hour
	x	4	Number of hours of TV use
	$		Cost to run TV for 4 hours

Money amounts need to be written to two decimal places. You need to round $_____ up to $ _____.

So, it costs Kelly about $_____ for 4 hours of television.

Write a plan to solve each problem. Explain your thinking and show your calculations. Then solve the problem.

1. Paul's air conditioner uses 36 kilowatt-hours of electricity a day. He had it on for 6 days straight in July. Paul pays $0.13 a kilowatt-hour.

How much did he pay for those 6 days of air-conditioning?

_____

_____

_____

_____

_____

_____

_____

_____

_____

_____

2. Three classes are taking a field-trip. Mr. De Marco's class has 27 students. Ms. De Fabbia's class has 32 students. Mrs. Lawrence's class has 28 students. Each bus for their trip has 45 seats.

Can all three classes and their teachers fit in 2 buses?

_____

_____

_____

_____

_____

_____

_____

_____

_____

● Test-Taking Skill

Drawing a Picture to Rename Measures

Some problems require you to rename measures given as a fraction of one unit. You can find the information you need in a table. It often helps to draw a picture of the unit you are renaming.

Customary Units of Measure

Units of Length	Units of Capacity	Units of Mass
1 foot (ft) = 12 inches (in.)	1 cup (c) = 8 fluid ounces (fl oz)	1 pound (lb) = 16 ounces (oz)
1 yard (yd) = 36 inches	1 pint (pt) = 2 cups (c)	1 ton (T) = 2,000 pounds
1 yard = 3 feet	1 quart (qt) = 2 pints	
1 mile (mi) = 5,280 feet	1 gallon (gal) = 4 quarts	
1 mile = 1,760 yards		

Example

The soccer team brought $2\frac{1}{2}$ gallons of orange juice. Each player will get 1 pint of juice. How many players can have orange juice?

A. **Find the number of pints in a gallon.** If the table doesn't compare gallons and pints, find a unit that is compared to both gallons and pints.

Draw pictures of equivalent amounts of each of the units.

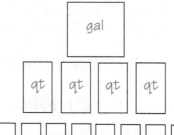

1 gal = _____ qt   1 qt = _____ pt

1 gal → 4 x 2 pt → _____ pt

B. **Decide whether to multiply or divide when you rename the units.**

- **Multiply** to rename a larger unit as a smaller unit.

- **Divide** to rename a smaller unit as a larger unit.

THINK: Pints are smaller, so there will be more pints than gallons.

To rename gallons as pints, you should _____ .

C. **Compute to solve the problem.**

Number of gallons x pints per gallon = total pints

$2\frac{1}{2}$ x   _____   =   _____

So, _____ players can have orange juice.

© 1999 Metropolitan Teaching & Learning Co.

1. Tara has $1\frac{1}{2}$ quarts of apple cider. How many cups can she serve?

Step 1: Find the number of cups in a quart. Draw a picture if it helps you.

1 qt = _____ pt   1 pt = _____ c

1 qt → 2 x 2 c → _____ c

Step 2: Decide whether to multiply or divide when you rename the units.

THINK: There will be more cups than quarts.

To rename quarts as cups, you should _____.

Step 3: Compute to solve the problem.

Number of quarts x cups per quart = total cups

_____   x   _____   =   _____

So, Tara can serve _____ cups of apple cider.

2. A window is 76 inches high. Will a curtain $6\frac{1}{2}$ ft long cover the window?

Step 1: Find the number of inches in a foot.

Draw a picture if it helps you.   1 ft = _____ in.

Step 2: Decide whether to multiply or divide to rename the units.

THINK: There will be fewer feet than inches.

To rename inches as feet, you should _____.

Step 3: Compute to rename the measure.

Number of inches ÷ inches per foot = total feet

_____   ÷   _____   = $6\frac{1}{3}$

Compare the measures. $6\frac{1}{3}$ ft < $6\frac{1}{2}$ ft

So, the curtain _____ cover the window.

PRACTICE

Solve. Use the table of measures to find the information you
need. Draw pictures if they help you.

Customary Units of Measure

Units of Length	Units of Capacity	Units of Mass
1 foot (ft) = 12 inches (in.)	1 cup (c) = 8 fluid ounces (fl oz)	1 pound (lb) = 16 ounces (oz)
1 yard (yd) = 36 inches	1 pint (pt) = 2 cups	1 ton (T) = 2,000 pounds
1 yard = 3 feet	1 quart (qt) = 2 pints	
1 mile (mi) = 5,280 feet	1 gallon = 4 quarts	
1 mile = 1,760 yards		

3. Janine has $\frac{2}{3}$ ft of red ribbon.
   How many inches of trim can
   she sew with the ribbon?

   _____

4. Kelly's favorite tree is 22 ft high.
   Will an $8\frac{1}{3}$ -yd ladder reach the
   top of the tree?

   _____

5. Gina is installing a TV cable
   $5\frac{1}{3}$ yd long. How many feet will
   the cable stretch?

   _____

6. A truck can carry a maximum
   weight of $3\frac{1}{2}$ tons. Can it carry
   7,500 pounds of gravel?

   _____

7. Robert pours $4\frac{3}{4}$ qt of lemonade
   into cups. How many cups does
   he fill?

   _____

8. Joan built a fence 14 ft long. She
   charges for her work by the yard.
   How many yards long is the
   fence?

   _____

9. The road to Alec's house is
   $2\frac{1}{2}$ miles long. There are markers
   every 100 yards along the road.
   How many markers are there?

   _____

10. Two bags of flour sell for the
    same price. One weighs $1\frac{1}{4}$ lb,
    and the other weighs 22 oz.
    Which is the better buy?

    _____

● Multiplying and Dividing with Fractions

For problems 1–4, choose the best answer for each problem. In the answer section at the bottom of the page, fill in the box of your choice.

Customary Units of Measurements

Units of Length	Units of Capacity	Units of Mass
1 foot (ft) = 12 inches (in.)	1 cup (c) = 8 fluid ounces (fl oz)	1 pound (lb) = 16 ounces (oz)
1 yard (yd) = 36 inches	1 pint (pt) = 2 cups	1 ton (T) = 2,000 pounds
1 yard (yd) = 3 feet	1 quart (qt) = 2 pints	
1 mile (mi) = 5,280 feet	1 gallon (gal) = 4 quarts	
I mile = 1,760 yards		

1. How many pint bottles can be filled with 64 fl oz of water?

A 2 C 16

B 4 D 64

2. The gym teacher is marking off a $\frac{1}{2}$-mi track. How many yards long should the track be?

J 440 yd L 1,760 yd

K 880 yd M 3,520 yd

3. A length of fabric is $4\frac{1}{2}$ ft long and 50 inches wide. Which statement is true?

A It is wider than it is long.

B It is longer than it is wide.

C Its length equals its width.

D Its width is half its length.

4. Which of the following number sentences can you use to find the number of cups in 1 gallon?

J 2 x 2 = 4 cups

K 2 x 4 = 8 cups

L 2 x 2 x 4 = 16 cups

M 8 x 2 x 2 = 32 cups

Write About It
Write a plan for solving the following problem. Then solve.

5. Duane jumped $3\frac{3}{4}$ yd and Momo jumped 11 ft 5 in. Who jumped farther?

_____

_____

_____

_____

_____

_____

1. A ☐ B ☐ C ☐ D ☐   4. J ☐ K ☐ L ☐ M ☐

2. J ☐ K ☐ L ☐ M ☐

3. A ☐ B ☐ C ☐ D ☐

● Multiplying and Dividing with Fractions

Is the Computed Number the Answer?

When you compute to solve a problem, the result of the computation is often the answer. Sometimes, you must decide whether the computation gives the kind of answer you need.

Example 1

It takes $1\frac{1}{2}$ cups of flour to make one batch of muffins. How many batches of muffins can you make with 5 cups of flour?

A. Divide the total amount of flour by the amount it takes to make one batch of muffins.

$5 \div$ _____ = _____

B. Reread the problem to determine if the quotient is the answer to the problem.

THINK: The problem asks how many *batches* you can make.

Does it make sense to have $3\frac{1}{3}$ batches of muffins? _____

So, $3\frac{1}{3}$ batches of muffins is the answer to the problem.

Example 2

A storm is threatening an island. Rescue boats can carry 8 people at a time. How many boats will the 43 people on the island need?

Step 1: Divide the total number of people by the number of people per boat.

$43 \div$ _____ = _____

Step 2: Reread the problem. Is the quotient the answer to the problem?

THINK: **Does it make sense to have $5\frac{3}{8}$ boats? _____**

Step 3: If the quotient doesn't answer the problem sensibly, round up or down.

THINK: All the people need boats, so you need to round up.

Round the quotient up to the next whole number.

So, the people on the island will need _____ boats.

GUIDED PRACTICE

1. Maria needs 15 quarts of fruit punch for a party. The punch is sold in 2-quart bottles. How many bottles should she buy?

   Step 1: Divide the total number of quarts by the number of quarts per bottle.

   $$15 \div \underline{\hspace{1.5cm}} = \underline{\hspace{1.5cm}}$$

   Step 2: Reread the problem to determine whether the quotient is the correct answer.

   Can Maria buy $7\frac{1}{2}$ bottles of punch? \underline{\hspace{2.5cm}}

   Step 3: If the quotient doesn't answer the problem sensibly, round up or down.

   THINK: Maria needs 15 quarts, so I need to round up.

   Round the quotient up to the next whole number.

   Maria should buy \underline{\hspace{1.5cm}} **bottles of punch.**

2. A recipe calls for 4 oz of chicken per person served. How many people can Rue serve if she has 18 oz of chicken?

   Step 1: Divide the total ounces of chicken by the ounces per serving.

   $$18 \div \underline{\hspace{1.5cm}} = \underline{\hspace{1.5cm}}$$

   Step 2: Reread the problem to determine whether the quotient is the correct answer.

   Can Rue serve $4\frac{1}{2}$ people? \underline{\hspace{2cm}}

   Step 3: If the quotient doesn't answer the problem sensibly, round up or down.

   THINK: Each person needs a whole serving, so I need to round down.

   Round the quotient down to the next whole number.

   So, Rue can serve \underline{\hspace{1.5cm}} **people.**

PRACTICE

Decide which kind of answer makes the most sense for each
problem. Then solve.

3. **Alina is sewing shirts. She has
8 yards of fabric. If 1 shirt takes
$2\frac{1}{2}$ yd of fabric, how many shirts
can she make?**

_____

4. **A video store is moving and
packing its tapes into boxes. Each
box holds 80 videos. How many
boxes are needed for the store's
5,432 tapes?**

_____

5. **Juice boxes come in packages of 3
boxes each. How many packages
should Mr. Lopez buy if he wants
1 box for each of his 26 scouts?**

_____

6. **The Juice Bar gives customers 1
free drink for every 5 drinks they
buy in one month. How many
free drinks can Tim get if he buys
17 drinks this month?**

_____

7. **Eddie has 245 baseball cards.
Each page in his binder can hold
9 cards. How many pages does
Eddie need for all of his cards?**

_____

8. **A space taxi uses 6 gallons of fuel
for each passenger it carries
between stations. If the taxi has
35 gallons of fuel, how many
passengers can it carry?**

_____

9. **After their matches, 4 soccer
teams have pizza delivered. They
have 18 pizzas to share. How
many pizzas can each team have?**

_____

10. **A factory produces a new car
every $3\frac{1}{2}$ hours. How many cars
does the factory produce in a
40-hour week?**

_____

● Multiplying and Dividing with Fractions

For problems 1–6, choose the best solution for each problem. In the answer section at the bottom of the page, fill in the box of your choice.

1. A bus holds 44 passengers. How many buses are needed to take 286 people on a trip?

   A 6   C 7
   B $6\frac{1}{2}$ D $7\frac{1}{2}$

2. Luis feeds his puppy 4 oz of food at each meal. How many meals can Luis give the puppy from a 50-oz bag of food?

   J 12   L 13
   K $12\frac{1}{2}$ M 46

3. A restaurant owner is feeding 250 people. She needs a slice of pie for each person. Each pie is cut into 8 slices. How many pies should she order?

   A 16   C 32
   B 31   D 125

4. A jogger runs 4 days a week. This week, she ran 15 miles. What was the average number of miles she ran per day?

   J 3   L 4
   K $3\frac{3}{4}$ M 9

5. A truck can hold 4,000 lb. Each box of machine parts weighs 35 lb. How many boxes can the truck hold?

   A 14   C $114\frac{1}{3}$
   B 114   D 115

6. It takes 3 people to crew a sailing boat in a contest. How many boats can a club enter in the contest if there are 26 members?

   J 8   L 9
   K $8\frac{2}{3}$ M 23

Write About It

Write a plan for solving the following problem. Then solve.

7. A carpenter bought a board that was 10 ft long. He plans to cut it into shelves that are $1\frac{1}{2}$ feet long. How many shelves can he make?

   _____

   _____

   _____

   _____

   _____

   _____

   _____

1. A ☐ B ☐ C ☐ D ☐

2. J ☐ K ☐ L ☐ M ☐

3. A ☐ B ☐ C ☐ D ☐

4. J ☐ K ☐ L ☐ M ☐

5. A ☐ B ☐ C ☐ D ☐

6. J ☐ K ☐ L ☐ M ☐

Using Models

In some problems, you'll have to divide whole numbers by fractions. You may find it helpful to use a model.

Example 1

A box contains 3 cups of cereal. If one serving of cereal is $\frac{3}{4}$ cup, how many servings does the box contain?

A. Draw three rectangles to represent 3 cups.

B. The divisor, $\frac{3}{4}$, is in fourths. So, divide the rectangles into fourths.

C. Count how many groups of $\frac{3}{4}$ fit into the rectangles.

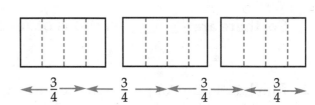

How many groups of $\frac{3}{4}$ fit?

_____ **groups**

So, the box contains _____ servings.

Example 2

Mr. Woo has 4 ft of aluminum foil. He wants to cut pieces that are $\frac{1}{3}$ ft long. How many pieces can he cut?

Step 1: Draw four rectangles to represent 4 feet.

Step 2: The divisor, $\frac{1}{3}$, is in thirds.

Divide the rectangles into thirds.

Step 3: Count the number of thirds.

THINK: There are 3 pieces in each foot.

So, I can multiply 4 x 3.   4 x 3 = _____

So, Mr. Woo can cut _____ pieces.

● Dividing with Fractions

GUIDED PRACTICE

1. A wooden fence is 5 yd long. Each section is $\frac{1}{2}$ yd long.
   How many sections of fence are there?

   Step 1: Draw five rectangles to represent 5 yards.

   Step 2: Divide the rectangles into halves.

   Step 3: Count the number of halves.

   THINK: There are 2 sections in each yard.

   So, I can multiply 5 x 2.   5 x 2 = _____

   So, there are _____ sections of fence.

2. Rita has 4 pints of juice. One serving is $\frac{2}{3}$ pt. How many
   servings of juice does she have?

   Step 1: Draw four rectangles to represent 4 pints.

   Step 2: The divisor, $\frac{2}{3}$, is in thirds. So, divide the rectangles into thirds.

   Step 3: Count how many groups of $\frac{2}{3}$ fit into the rectangles.

   How many groups of $\frac{2}{3}$ fit? _____ groups

   So, Rita has _____ servings of juice.

PRACTICE

Draw a model to help you solve each problem. Then solve.

3. Dave uses $\frac{1}{2}$ cup of sugar when he makes 1 pitcher of iced tea. How many pitchers of iced tea can he make with 3 cups of sugar?

_____

4. Jed has 2 cups of applesauce. The dessert cups hold $\frac{2}{3}$ cup each. How many dessert cups can he fill with the applesauce?

_____

5. Lisette has 9 yards of ribbon. She decides to cut the ribbon into strips $\frac{3}{4}$ of a yard long to make streamers for a party. How many streamers can she cut?

_____

6. Nina has a 5-lb bag of peanuts. She can fit $\frac{5}{8}$ lb into one plastic snack bag. How many snack bags can she fill with peanuts?

_____

● Dividing with Fractions

TEST-TAKING PRACTICE

Choose the best solution for each problem. In the answer section at the bottom of the page, fill in the box of your choice.

1. A banner is 7 ft long. Lita is attaching stickers every $\frac{1}{3}$ ft. How many stickers does she need for the whole banner?

A $\frac{3}{7}$	**C** 7
B $2\frac{1}{3}$	**D** 21

2. A track is 2 mi long. It has markers posted every $\frac{1}{4}$ mi. How many markers does it have?

J 2	**L** 8
K 4	**M** 10

3. A thermos holds 6 c of liquid. The drinking cup holds $\frac{3}{4}$ c. How many times can the drinking cup be filled from the thermos?

A 6	**C** 8
B 7	**D** 9

4. A recipe calls for $\frac{2}{3}$ c of raisins per serving. How many servings can Elena make if she has 4 c of raisins?

J 6	**L** 9
K 8	**M** 12

5. Janus has 4 m of string. He must cut the string into $\frac{2}{5}$-m pieces for a science project. How many pieces can he cut?

A 8	**C** 16
B 10	**D** 20

Write About It

Write a plan for solving the following problem. Then solve.

6. A truck holds 5 T of coal when full. If it delivers loads of $\frac{5}{6}$ T each, how many loads can a full truck deliver?

    _____

    _____

    _____

    _____

    _____

    _____

1. A ☐ B ☐ C ☐ D ☐   4. J ☐ K ☐ L ☐ M ☐

2. J ☐ K ☐ L ☐ M ☐   5. A ☐ B ☐ C ☐ D ☐

3. A ☐ B ☐ C ☐ D ☐

● Dividing with Fractions

Explaining the Problem in Your Own Words

Sometimes you can solve a problem more easily if you show the information in another way. Rewrite the problem in your own words as a word equation.

Example

Phil bought 6 blank cassette tapes.
The total cost was $21.
What was the cost of one blank tape?

A. Write a word equation first. Here's one way.

> Total cost ÷ Number of tapes = Cost of one tape

B. The word equation has three pieces of information.

Decide which information you know and which you don't know.

Number of tapes	⇒	6
Cost of one tape	⇒	don't know
Total cost	⇒	$21

C. Rewrite your word equation as a mathematical equation.

If you know a number, use it.

If you don't know a number, use a variable to show you want to find that number.

Total cost	**÷**	**Number of tapes**	**=**	**Cost of one tape**
↓		↓		↓
21	÷	6	=	n

D. Find the value of the variable.

$$21 \div 6 = n$$
$$3.50 = n$$

So, one tape cost $ _____ .

1. Will bought 3 T-shirts. Each T-shirt had the same price.
   The total price was $46.50. What was the price of each T-shirt?

   a. Write a word equation. Here's one way.

   Total price ÷ Number of shirts = Price of one shirt

   b. Write what you know and don't know. Then write a math equation by using that information and a word equation.

   Number of shirts   ⇒   3
   Price of one shirt   ⇒   don't know
   Total price   ⇒ $46.50

   Total price   ÷   Number of shirts   =   Price of one shirt

   _____ ÷   3   =   _____

   c. Find the value of the variable.

   $p =$ _____

   So, each shirt cost $ _____ .

2. At the carnival, Latoya gave her sister half of the tickets
   she had. Latoya then had 18 tickets. How many tickets did
   Latoya have at first?

   a. Write a word equation.

   Total tickets ÷ 2 = Tickets Latoya has left.

   b. Write what you know and don't know. Then write a math equation by using that information and a variable.

   Number of tickets to sister   ⇒   half the total
   Total tickets   ⇒   don't know
   Tickets left   ⇒   18

   $t ÷$ _____ = _____

   c. Find the value of the variable.

   $t =$ _____

   So, Latoya had _____ at first.

Name _____

PRACTICE

Write a word equation for each problem. Write what you know and don't know. Then write a math equation that has a variable. Find the value of the variable to solve the problem.

3. Maria has 140 books to pack in boxes. Each packing box can hold 20 books. How many boxes will she need?

_____

_____

_____

4. Otis is reading a book that has 275 pages. He has read 147 pages so far. How many more pages must he read to finish the book?

_____

_____

_____

5. The swim team is washing cars to raise money for a trip. The trip will cost $350. The members will earn $5 for each car wash. How many cars must the members wash to raise all the money?

_____

_____

_____

6. Ms. Lopez arranged her campers in groups of exactly 4 for a nature project. She was able to make 8 groups. How many campers does she have in all?

_____

_____

_____

7. Jamal went to the movies with $15. When he came home, he had $2.50. How much did he spend at the movies?

_____

_____

_____

8. Luz, Rita, and Sue found a box of seashells in their grandmother's attic. The box held 72 shells. They decided to share them equally. How many shells did each girl get?

_____

_____

_____

● Variables and Expressions

Choose the best equation for solving each problem. Fill in the answer box of your choice in the section at the bottom of the page.

1. The library charges 5¢ per day for books that are late. Raul paid a fine of 35¢ for one book he returned. How many days late was the book?

   A $35 - d = 5$ C $d + 5 = 35$
   B $5 \times d = 35$ D $d \div 5 = 35$

2. Tom can fit 8 video games in a shoe box. How many shoe boxes will he need if he has 40 games?

   J $b + 8 = 40$ L $8 \times b = 40$
   K $40 - b = 8$ M $b \div 8 = 40$

3. Mrs. Ruiz is planning her flower garden. She wants to plant 96 tulip bulbs in 6 rows. How many bulbs should she plant in each row?

   A $96 + 6 = 102$ C $96 \times 6 = 576$
   B $96 - 6 + 90$ D $96 \div 6 = 16$

4. Loretta earns $4.50 per hour to baby-sit children. Last Saturday she baby-sat for 5 hours. How much money did Loretta earn?

   J $4.50 + 5 = 4.55$
   K $4.50 \times 5 = 22.50$
   L $4.50 - 5 = 4.55$
   M $4.50 \div 5 = 0.90$

Solve each problem. Fill in the answer box of your choice in the section at the bottom of the page.

5. Darryl gave half his baseball cards to his brother. He has 48 cards left. How many did he have before he gave some to his brother?

   A 24 cards   C 46 cards
   B 100 cards   D 96 cards

6. Trini bought a CD at the mall. She gave the clerk $20 and got $7.45 in change. How much did the CD cost?

   J $12.55   L $5.12
   K $8.55   M $12.45

Write About It

Write a plan for solving this problem.

7. Felicia bought 2 pens that were the same price and a notebook that cost $3. Her total bill was $5.50. What was the price of one pen?

   _____

   _____

   _____

   _____

   _____

   _____

1. A ▢ B ▢ C ▢ D ▢   4. J ▢ K ▢ L ▢ M ▢

2. J ▢ K ▢ L ▢ M ▢   5. A ▢ B ▢ C ▢ D ▢

3. A ▢ B ▢ C ▢ D ▢   6. J ▢ K ▢ L ▢ M ▢

● Variables and Expressions

Drawing a Number Line

Drawing a number line can help you solve problems that use positive and negative integers.

Example 1

When Jake woke up on Monday, the temperature was ⁻8 degrees. By noon, the temperature had risen 6 degrees. What was the temperature at noon?

A. **Decide how to solve the problem.**

I should count up _____ degrees from ⁻8°C.

B. Draw a number line.

Mark the line with a dot to show ⁻8°C.

C. Use the number line to solve the problem.

Begin at the dot you have drawn, then move 6 places to the right.

At which number do you end up? _____

So, the temperature at noon was _____ °C.

Example 2

On Tuesday morning, the temperature was ⁻2°C. By noon, it had dropped 3 degrees. What was the temperature at noon?

Step 1: Decide how to solve the problem.

I should count down _____ degrees from ⁻2°C.

Step 2: Use a number line to solve the problem.

Mark the line with a dot to show ⁻2°C, then move 3 places to the left.

At which number do you end up? _____

So, the temperature at noon was _____ °C.

● Adding and Subtracting Integers

GUIDED PRACTICE

1. At noon, the thermometer read ⁻4°C. At sunset, the temperature was ⁻10°C. How many degrees had the temperature dropped?

   Step 1: Decide how to solve the problem.

   I should find the change from _____ °C to _____ °C.

   Step 2: Draw a number line.

   Mark the line with dots to show ⁻4°C and ⁻10°C.

   Step 3: Use the number line to solve the problem.

   Count the spaces from ⁻4°C to ⁻10°C.

   There are _____ spaces. You need to count down (to the left).

   So, the temperature had dropped _____ degrees.

2. Mike measured the temperature of a liquid in a science experiment and found it was ⁻1°C. He heated the liquid to a temperature of ⁺3°C. By how many degrees did the temperature of the liquid change? Did it increase or decrease?

   Step 1: Decide how to solve the problem.

   I should find the change from _____ °C to _____ °C.

   Step 2: Draw a number line.

   Mark the line with dots to show ⁻1°C and ⁺3°C.

   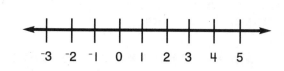

   Step 3: Use the number line to solve the problem.

   Count the spaces from ⁻1°C to 3°C.

   There are _____ spaces. You need to count up (to the right).

   So, the temperature changed by _____ degrees.

   It _____.

PRACTICE

Mark the number lines to solve each problem.

3. How many degrees warmer is a temperature of
   $^-3°C$ than a temperature of $^-8°C$?

_____

4. The temperatures of two liquids in a science
   experiment are $^-6°C$ and $^+1°C$. What is the difference
   between the two temperatures?

_____

5. When Paul left for school it was $^+5°C$. During the
   afternoon the temperature dropped 7 degrees. What
   was the temperature when Paul came home from
   school?

_____

6. Sue's town is 7 degrees warmer than Bob's town, where
   the temperature is $^-16°C$. What is the temperature in
   Sue's town?

_____

7. On Monday it was $^-10°C$. The temperature rose
   12 degrees on Tuesday and then dropped 5 degrees on
   Wednesday. What was the temperature on Wednesday?

_____

● Adding and Subtracting Integers

Choose the best answer for each problem. Fill in the answer box of your choice in the section at the bottom of the page.

1. **Which problem is shown on this number line?**

   A $2 - 5 = n$ C $2 - 3 = n$
   B $^-3 - 2 = n$ D $^-3 + 2 = n$

2. **Which problem is shown on this number line?**

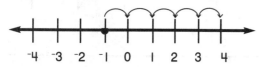

   J $4 - 1 = n$ L $4 - ^-1 = n$
   K $^-1 - 4 = n$ M $^-1 + 5 = n$

3. **Which problem is shown on this number line?**

   A $^-3 - 1 = n$ C $^-3 - 4 = n$
   B $1 - 4 = n$ D $^-3 + 1 = n$

4. **The temperature of a liquid was -3°C. The temperature was increased by 10 degrees. What was the final temperature of the liquid?**

   J -13°C   L 7°C
   K 3°C   M 13°C

5. **The temperature at 6 A.M. was -12°C. During the day, the temperature rose 8 degrees. What was the temperature at the end of the day?**

   A -20°C   C 4°C
   B -4°C   D 20°C

Write About It

Explain how you could use a number line to solve the following problem. Then solve.

6. **The temperature at dawn was $^+3$°C. During the day, it dropped 7 degrees. What was the temperature at the end of the day?**

_____

_____

_____

_____

_____

1. A ☐   B ☐   C ☐   D ☐   4. J ☐   K ☐   L ☐   M ☐

2. J ☐   K ☐   L ☐   M ☐   5. A ☐   B ☐   C ☐   D ☐

3. A ☐   B ☐   C ☐   D ☐

• Adding and Subtracting Integers

Test-Taking Skill: Visualizing the Problem

If you have trouble understanding a problem, it can help to show the information in the problem a different way. Here are some ideas.

- Make a visual model, such as a diagram, a drawing, or a number line.
- Write a word equation or a number equation for the problem.
- Make a table to find a pattern.

Example 1

A swimming pool is 24 feet wide and 50 feet long. There is a row of blue tiles along each side. If there are 2 tiles every foot, how many tiles are there?

A 148 feet   **B** 148 tiles   **C** 296 feet   **D** 296 tiles

THINK: Find the perimeter first, and then multiply by 2 to find the number of tiles. I can **make a diagram** to show the perimeter.

50 ft

24 ft

The perimeter is _____ ft, so the correct choice is _____.

Example 2

A pancake recipe calls for 1 quart of milk to make 24 pancakes. A camp cook wants to make 96 pancakes. How many quarts of milk does he need?

A 1 quart   **B** 24 pancakes   **C** 3 quarts   **D** 4 quarts

THINK: I can **make a table** to find the number of quarts needed to make 96 pancakes.

Number of quarts of milk	1	2	3	4
Number of pancakes	24	48	72	96

The cook needs _____ of milk, so the correct choice is _____.

● Test-Taking Skill

Use the extra space on this page to show the problem in another way. Then solve the problem. In the answer section at the bottom of this page, fill in the box of your choice.

1. Lou planted 3 rows of vegetables. He planted beets 2 inches apart. He put the peas 5 inches apart. He left 8 inches between every two tomato plants. **At how many inches did all three rows line up?**

   A 8 inches   **C** 16 inches
   B 10 inches   **D** 40 inches

2. The Radio Station has 982 CDs. They bought a CD rack with 8 sections. Each section holds 75 CDs. **How many CDs do not fit in the rack?**

   J 75 CDs   **L** 382 CDs
   K 300 CDs   **M** 600 CDs

3. Masao walks to school and back home every day. The school is 4.7 kilometers from his house. **How many kilometers does he walk in 5 days?**

   A 4.7 km   **C** 23.5 km
   B 9.4 km   **D** 47 km

4. Teo wants to buy a new coat that costs $79. He can earn $6.50 per hour baby-sitting. **How many hours will he need to baby-sit to buy the coat?**

   J 5 hours   **L** 12 hours
   K 10 hours   **M** 13 hours

1. A ☐ B ☐ C ☐ D ☐   4. J ☐ K ☐ L ☐ M ☐

2. J ☐ K ☐ L ☐ M ☐

3. A ☐ B ☐ C ☐ D ☐

● Test-Taking Skill

Writing Equal Ratios

You can solve some problems by showing information as a number sentence with two equal ratios. Using words may help you set up the two ratios so that their numerators and denominators match.

Example

Tracy drew this design for a sweater pattern. She used a scale of 3 mm on her drawing for every 10 mm on the actual sweater. In the drawing, the width of the *T* measures 27 millimeters. What is the actual width of the *T*?

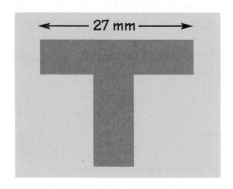

A. One of the ratios is the scale.

In words, describe the scale Tracy used.

In the drawing, _____ mm stands for _____ mm on the sweater.

B. Write the scale as a ratio.

$$\dfrac{\text{_____ in the drawing}}{\text{_____ on the sweater}}$$

C. Complete the number sentence. Write the second ratio so that the numerator and denominator match the first ratio. Use a symbol such as w for the unknown measurement.

$$\dfrac{\text{_____}}{\text{_____}} = \dfrac{\text{_____ mm in drawing}}{w \text{ mm on sweater}}$$

D. Now, solve the number sentence.

$3 \times w = 10 \times 27$

$3 \times w = 270$

$w = 90$

So, the actual width of the *T* on the sweater is _____ mm.

GUIDED PRACTICE

One centimeter on this map is equal to 5 kilometers actual distance on the ground.

1. On the map, the distance from Oak Grove to Blue Lake is 3 centimeters. What is the actual distance?

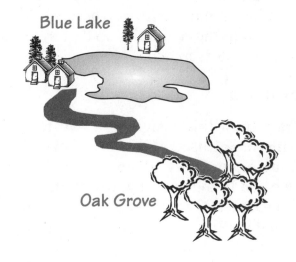

Blue Lake

Oak Grove

   a. In this problem, the map unit is different from the actual unit.

   Write a word sentence to describe the map scale.

   _____

   _____

   _____

   b. Write a ratio for the map scale.

   on the map   _____
   _____
   actual distance   _____

   c. Remember to match the first ratio when you write the second ratio. Choose a letter to represent the unknown number.

   Write a ratio for the distance between Oak Grove and Blue Lake.

   _____

   d. Use the two ratios to write a number sentence, or proportion. Then solve.

   _____

   So, the actual distance between Blue Lake and

   Oak Grove is _____.

Name_____

PRACTICE

For problems 2 and 3, write a number sentence with equal ratios. Be sure the numerators and denominators match. Then solve the proportion to answer the question.

2. **Lauren can string 2 beads every 9 seconds. How many beads can she string in 45 seconds?**

_____

_____

3. Nick is making a scale drawing of his garden. In his drawing, 1 centimeter stands for 4 meters on the ground.

GARDEN

   a. **The garden is 28 meters long. What length will Nick draw the length of the garden?**

_____

   b. **Nick drew a 3-cm line to show the width of the garden. How wide is the garden?**

_____

Solve . . . .

4. Grapefruit are priced at 3 for $2. **How many grapefruit can you buy for $14?**

_____

5. On a map, 2 centimeters stands for 5 kilometers. The bicycle path Angie wants to take is 16 cm long on the map. **How long is the bicycle path?**

_____

6. In basketball practice, Rashid shoots 3 foul shots every 40 seconds. **How many foul shots does he shoot in 120 seconds?**

_____

7. Rosalinda is on the volleyball team. On average, she serves 5 times every 3 games. **How many times does she serve in 15 games?**

_____

TEST-TAKING PRACTICE

Choose the best answer for each problem. In the answer section at the bottom of the page, fill in the box of your choice.

Use this problem for items 1–3.

Ruth is making yellow and green striped banners. She uses 7 green stripes for every 6 yellow stripes. How many yellow stripes does she need if she has 35 green stripes?

1. **Which ratio describes the proportion of stripes Ruth uses?**

   A 7 green/6 yellow
   B 6 green/7 yellow
   C 7 green/13 yellow
   D 6 green/13 yellow

2. **Which pair of equal ratios can be solved to find the number of yellow stripes Ruth needs?**

   J $\frac{6}{7} = \frac{35}{y}$ L $\frac{7}{6} = \frac{35}{y}$

   K $\frac{6}{35} = \frac{7}{y}$ M $\frac{y}{35} = \frac{7}{6}$

3. **How many yellow stripes does Ruth need if she has 35 green stripes?**

   A 49 yellow stripes
   B 42 yellow stripes
   C 36 yellow stripes
   D 30 yellow stripes

4. **At a book fair, hardback books are priced at 3 for $5. Adam bought 18 books. How much money did Adam spend?**

   J $15   K $18
   L $24   M $30

5. **On a map, 1 inch stands for 8 miles. The distance from Big River to Little River is 32 miles. How far is it between the two towns on the map?**

   A 4 miles   C 24 inches
   B 4 inches   D 32 inches

Write About It

6. Explain how you would set up two equal ratios to solve this problem.

   Greg uses 9 quarts of water for every 1 sack of concrete mix. How many quarts of water will he need for 5 sacks of concrete?

   _____

   _____

   _____

   _____

---

1. A ☐ B ☐ C ☐ D ☐   4. J ☐ K ☐ L ☐ M ☐

2. J ☐ K ☐ L ☐ M ☐   5. A ☐ B ☐ C ☐ D ☐

3. A ☐ B ☐ C ☐ D ☐

● Ratios

Name_____

Making a Rate Table

In many problems, you are given a rate, such as dollars per hour or gallons per mile. A table can help you see the relationship between the two units that form a rate.

Example 1

One gallon of gasoline costs $1.32. Jonathan has $5. About how many gallons of gasoline can he buy?

A. Make a rate table by adding $1.32 again and again.

Look for a cost that is close to $5. Then read the number of gallons.

Exactly _____ gallons of gasoline cost $5.28.

B. Reread the problem to be sure of the question you need to answer.

Jonathan can buy a little less than _____ gallons of gasoline.

Gallons	Cost
1	$1.32
2	$2.64
3	$3.96
4	$5.28
5	$6.60
6	$7.92
7	$9.24

Example 2

Jonathan's car gets 25 miles per gallon of gasoline. About how many gallons of gas will he use on a 219-mile trip?

Step 1: Complete the table.

Gal	1	2	3	4	5	6	7	8	9	10
Miles										

Step 2: Look for the number of miles closest to 219. Estimate the number of gallons of gasoline needed for a 219-mile trip.

Jonathan will use almost _____ gallons of gasoline on a 219-mile trip.

© 1999 Metropolitan Teaching & Learning Co.

● Finding Rates

Make and use tables to solve these problems.

1. Lian earns $18 an hour. About how long does it take her to earn $100?

   a. **Complete this table to show how much Lian earns for multiple hours of work.**

Hours	1	2						
Earnings	$18							

   b. **Read the table. How much does Lian earn in an 8-hour workday?**

   _____

   c. **Use the table to estimate. About how long does it take Lian to earn $100?**

   _____

2. Hideo filled $1\frac{1}{2}$ baskets with cherries in the first hour. How long will it take him to fill 10 baskets?

   a. **Label each column in the table. Then complete the table.**

   b. **How many baskets can Hideo fill in 6 hours?**

   _____

   c. **Estimate how long will it take Hideo to fill 10 baskets.**

   _____

   _____

PRACTICE

For problems 3–6, use the outline provided to make a rate table. Use the table to solve the problems.

3. When he is at rest, Neil's heart beats 65 times each minute. How many times does his heart beat in 3 minutes?

   a. Fill in the table at the right.

   b. Solve.

   In 3 minutes, Neil's heart beats _____ times.

4. **About how many minutes does it take Neil's heart to beat 500 times?**

   _____

5. **Does Neil's heart beat more than 300 times or fewer than 300 times in 5 minutes?**

   _____

6. **Neil counted his heartbeats to estimate the length of a television commercial. His heart beat 265 times. About how long was the commercial?**

   _____

Solve . . . .

7. Willa's grocery bill last week was $57.83. **At $12 an hour, about how many hours did she have to work to pay for last week's groceries?**

   _____

   _____

8. Josh sells ice cream. There are 16 cones in one box. **If he sells 184 cones in a week, about how many boxes does he sell?**

   _____

9. Rivka earns $6.75 an hour as a painter's assistant. **If a new tarp costs $40.00, how many hours will she have to work to buy it?**

   _____

10. Elizabeth earns $12.25 an hour. **Does she earn enough in an 8-hour day to buy a coat that costs $89?**

    _____

● Finding Rates

Choose the best answer for each problem. In the answer
section at the bottom of the page, fill in the box of your choice.

Lin's car can travel 22 miles on 1 gallon
of gasoline. **Complete and use this rate
table to answer questions 1–4.**

Gallons	Miles
1	22
2	44
3	
4	
5	
6	
7	
8	
9	
10	
11	
12	
13	
14	

1. **Lin has 6 gallons of gasoline.
   How many miles can she drive?**

   A 66 miles   **C** 132 miles
   B 120 miles   **D** 220 miles

2. **Lin drove 180 miles. About how
   many gallons of gas did she use?**

   J about 4 gallons
   K about 8 gallons
   L about 10 gallons
   M about 14 gallons

3. **Lin's gas tank holds 14 gallons of
   gas. How far can Lin drive if she
   has a full tank of gas?**

   A 22 miles   **C** 220 miles
   B 88 miles   **D** 308 miles

4. **Lin's 14-gallon gas tank is half
   full. If she drives 130 miles to
   visit her aunt, which statement is
   true?**

   J Lin will run out of gas.
   K Lin will have 5 gallons of
       gas left.
   L Lin will not run out of gas.
   M Lin's aunt will give her
       money for gas.

Write About It
Explain how you would set up a rate
table and use it to solve this problem.

5. **Jordan jogs 16 miles each week.
   Does he jog more or less than
   80 miles a month?**

   _____

   _____

   _____

   _____

   _____

1. A ☐   B ☐   C ☐   D ☐   4. J ☐   K ☐   L ☐   M ☐

2. J ☐   K ☐   L ☐   M ☐

3. A ☐   B ☐   C ☐   D ☐

       ● Finding Rates

Name _____

What Are the Units?

Answering a rate problem often means finding the *unit rate*. A *unit rate* compares units of one kind to a *single* unit of another kind: for example, miles per gallon or ticket sales per week.

Example

Beverly earned $104 in 4 hours. What was Beverly's rate of pay?

A. Find the unit rate to give the answer to the problem

Use the two kinds of units given in the problem to complete this sentence.

The unit rate is the number of _____ for 1 _____.

Write the unit rate as a ratio. Use x for the amount you do not know.

$$\frac{\text{\_\_\_\_\_ dollars}}{\text{\_\_\_\_\_ hour}}$$

B. Use the numbers given in the problem to write an equal ratio. Match the numerators and the denominators to complete a proportion.

$$\frac{x \text{ dollars}}{1 \text{ hour}} = \frac{104 \text{_____}}{4 \text{_____}}$$

C. Solve the proportion to find the unit rate. Then answer the question.

$$x = \text{_____}$$

Beverly's rate of pay was _____.

GUIDED PRACTICE

1. Joyce ate 75 grapes in 5 minutes. How many grapes did she eat per minute?

   a. Use the units in the problem. Complete this sentence.

   The unit rate is the number of _____ for 1 _____.

   b. Write the unit rate as a ratio.

   c. Write the unit ratio and Joyce's eating ratio as a proportion.

   d. Solve the proportion, and write a sentence to answer the question.

   How many grapes did Joyce eat per minute?

   _____

2. Will drove 180 miles in 4 hours. At what rate did he drive?

   a. Complete this sentence:

   The unit rate is the number of _____ for _____.

   b. What is the ratio for the unit rate?

   c. In what units will the answer for this problem be expressed?

   _____

   d. Answer the question.

   Will drove at _____.

PRACTICE

For problems 3–6, complete the sentence about the unit rate.
Then solve.

3. Postcards are priced at 5 for $2.00. What is the unit price?

   a. The unit rate is the number of

   _____ for 1 _____.

   b. The unit price is:

   _____

4. Sharon read 96 pages in 2 hours. At what rate did she read?

   a. The unit rate is the number of

   _____ for 1 _____.

   b. The unit rate is:

   _____

5. Angela spent $735 on a 7-day vacation. What was her daily spending rate?

   a. The unit rate is the number of

   _____ for 1 _____.

   b. The unit rate is:

   _____

6. Leroy spent $96 for 6 bouquets of flowers. What is the cost per unit?

   a. The unit rate is the number of

   _____ for 1 _____.

   b. The unit price is:

   _____

Solve . . . .

7. Twelve muffins cost $5.40. What is the unit price?

   _____

8. George built 15 models in 6 days. At what rate did he build the models?

   _____

9. Karen wrapped 6 gifts in 30 minutes. At what rate did she wrap the gifts?

   _____

10. Ravi wrote 35 pages in 1 week. At what daily rate did he write?

   _____

Choose the best answer for each problem. In the answer section at the bottom of the page, fill in the box of your choice.

Use this problem for questions 1–3.

Ashraf walked 12 miles in 4 hours. At what rate did he walk?

1. **Which describes the unit rate?**

   A The number of miles walked each hour

   B The number of hours for each mile

   C The number of hours per mile for each hour

   D The number of hours per week for each mile

2. **Which unit will be used to express the rate at which Ashraf walked?**

   J miles   L miles per walk
   K hours   M miles per hour

3. **At what rate did Ashraf walk?**

   A 3 hours
   B 3 miles
   C 3 miles per hour
   D 3 miles per walk

4. **Stuffed animals are priced at 2 for $4.98. What is the unit price for the stuffed animals?**

   J $9.96 per stuffed animal
   K 4 per $9.96
   L 2.49 stuffed animals per dollar
   M $2.49 per stuffed animal

5. **Yolanda's long-distance call lasted 54 minutes and cost $6.48. What was the call's rate per minute?**

   A $0.01 per minute
   B $0.12 per minute
   C 54 minutes per hour
   D $349.92

Write About It

Explain how you would figure out which units to use for the answer to this problem.

6. **Steven paid $9.72 for a box of 12 die-cast cars. What was the unit price of the cars?**

   _____

   _____

   _____

   _____

1. A☐ B☐ C☐ D☐   4. J☐ K☐ L☐ M☐

2. J☐ K☐ L☐ M☐   5. A☐ B☐ C☐ D☐

3. A☐ B☐ C☐ D☐

Drawing a Number-Line Segment

You can use a number-line segment to help you estimate a percent of a number.

Example 1

About 75% of the members of the drama club were at last night's show. The drama club has 84 members. About how many club members were at the show?

A. Draw a number-line segment. Above the segment, label the endpoints 0 and 84. Below the segment, label the endpoints 0% and 100%.

```
0  10  20  30  40  50  60  70  80 84
0%                                100%
```

B. Think about the percents you know. Then write the percents below the number-line segment. First, write 50%. Then write 25% and 75%.

C. Use the model to estimate 75% of 84.

So, about _____ club members were at the show.

Example 2

About 20% of the members of the drama club were also members last year. Of the 84 members, about how many were members last year?

Step 1: Think about where 20% is located on the segment.

>   *THINK:* 20% is less than but close to 25%.

Step 2: Estimate the number that is above 20% on the number line.

So, about _____ members were in the club last year.

© 1999 Metropolitan Teaching & Learning Co.

GUIDED PRACTICE

You can use estimation to help you solve multiple-choice problems. Draw a percent model to help you solve the problems. Circle the correct answers.

1. Margie has a collection of 63 stuffed animals. She is planning to give 33% of them away. How many stuffed animals will she give away?

   A 21   C 42

   B 32   D 51

   a. Draw a number-line segment from 0 to 63. Below the line, label the endpoints 0% and 100%.

   b. Draw marks to show 33% and 67% ($\frac{1}{3}$ and $\frac{2}{3}$).

   c. Use the model to estimate 33% of 63. How many stuffed animals will Margie give away?

      A 21   C 42

      B 32   D 51

2. Trevor works 40 hours each week. His work for this week is 50% done. How many hours has Trevor worked?

   J 5   L 20

   K 10   M 30

   a. Draw and label a number-line segment.

   b. Draw a mark to show 50%.

   c. Estimate 50% of 40 to answer the question. How many hours has Trevor worked?

PRACTICE

Use the space provided to draw percent models. Circle the correct answers.

3. There were 36 people on a train. At the South End Station, 25% of them left the train. **How many people left the train?**

   A 9   B 18   C 25   D 32

4. There are 50 bulbs in a package. Doris is going to plant 50% of them in her front flower bed. **How many bulbs will she plant in the front flower bed?**

   J 10   K 15   L 25   M 35

5. Of the 56 lights on Elm Street, 75% are working. **How many lights are working?**

   A 18   B 28   C 42   D 50

Estimate the answer.

6. David has the signatures of 42 major-league football players. His favorite team has 67% of those 42 players. **About how many signatures are by members of David's favorite team?**

   _____

7. Ms. Evans had $72 in her purse. She gave 25% of her money to her daughter. **About how much money did Ms. Evans give her daughter?**

   _____

● Estimating Percents

For problems 1–6, choose the best answer for each problem. In the answer section at the bottom of the page, fill in the box of your choice.

1. Mandy earned $42. She wants to save 50% of her earnings. How much of the $42 should she save?

   A $7   C $14
   B $21   D $35

2. Hoshi needs 60 mg of vitamin C each day. He gets 25% of his vitamin C at breakfast. How many mg of vitamin C does he get at breakfast?

   J 15 mg   L 25 mg
   K 40 mg   M 52 mg

3. Nina bought 27 sweatshirts for her store. Of the sweatshirts, 33% were size large. How many were size large?

   A 3   C 9
   B 18   D 21

4. On a 44-question test Mark answered 75% of the questions correctly. How many questions did he answer correctly?

   J 8   L 15
   K 22   M 33

5. Of 62 band members, 50% are marching in a parade. How many band members are marching?

   A 21   C 31
   B 41   D 51

6. Pearl ordered 48 flowers. Of the flowers, 75% are daisies. How many are daisies?

   J 12   L 16
   K 27   M 36

Write About It
Explain how you could use a number-line segment to model this percent problem.

7. Len tried 68 foul shots. He made 25% of them. About how many shots did Len make?

   _____

   _____

   _____

   _____

   _____

   _____

   _____

   _____

1. A ☐ B ☐ C ☐ D ☐   4. J ☐ K ☐ L ☐ M ☐

2. J ☐ K ☐ L ☐ M ☐   5. A ☐ B ☐ C ☐ D ☐

3. A ☐ B ☐ C ☐ D ☐   6. J ☐ K ☐ L ☐ M ☐

● Estimating Percents

Deciding How to Estimate

Sometimes, an estimate is all you need to answer a question. If you know that $\frac{1}{4} = 25\%$, $\frac{1}{2} = 50\%$, and $\frac{3}{4} = 75\%$, you can solve many percent problems by estimating.

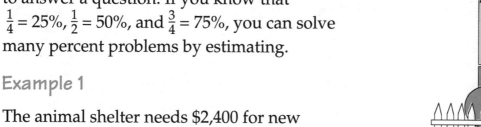

Example 1

The animal shelter needs \$2,400 for new fencing. So far, it has achieved 29% of its goal. About how much money has it raised so far?

29%

A. Use the fractions for 25%, 50%, and 75% as benchmarks.

29% is about 25%, or $\frac{1}{4}$.

B. Find $\frac{1}{4}$ of \$2,400 to estimate the amount of money raised so far.

$\frac{1}{4} \times 2,400 = 600$

C. Decide whether the amount the animal shelter has raised is greater than \$600 or less than \$600.

Because 25% is less than 29%, \$600 is less than the amount of money raised so far.

D. About how much money has the animal shelter raised so far?

The animal shelter has raised a little more than \$600 so far.

Example 2

The next month, the animal shelter raised \$715. Has it raised 50% of the money it needs yet?

Step 1: Estimate 50% of \$2,400.

$\frac{1}{2}$ of 2,400 = _____

Step 2: Calculate how much money has been raised.

\$600 + \$715 = \$ _____

So, the shelter _____ raised 50% of the money it needs.

● Estimating Percents

1. Of the 618 tickets sold for the matinee performance of *The Nutcracker*, about 46% were children's tickets. About how many children's tickets were sold?

   a. 46% is close to what fraction?

   46% is about _____ %, or _____.

   b. The number of tickets sold was about 600. Find the fractional part of 600.

   _____

   c. About how many children's tickets were sold?

   _____

2. For an evening performance of *The Nutcracker*, 780 tickets were sold. About 78% of the tickets sold were adult tickets. About how many adult tickets were sold?

   a. What fraction can you use to estimate 78%? _____

   b. Estimate the fractional part.

   _____

   c. About how many adult tickets were sold?

   _____

3. At the evening performance, 409 of the 1,189 seats were empty. Was the number of empty seats more or less than 25% of the seats?

   Estimate 25% of 1,189. _____

   So, the number of empty seats was

   _____ than 25% of the seats.

PRACTICE

Use the fractions for 25%, 50%, and 75%. Estimate to solve each problem.

4. Approximately 23% of the 156 people surveyed like Brand A chewing gum best. About how many people liked Brand A best?

_____

_____

5. There are 980 books to be sold at the library's book sale. About 55% of them are hardback books. About how many are hardback books?

_____

_____

6. Eve spent $156 on a dress and shoes. The dress cost 76% of the money. About how much did the dress cost?

_____

_____

7. Of the 84 people taking a science class, about 77% plan to go on the field trip. About how many people plan to go on the trip?

_____

_____

8. Mr. Mallory says that he spent 48% of his advertising budget on newspaper ads. If his advertising budget was $640, about how much did he spend on advertising?

_____

_____

9. Mrs. Johnson spent $278 to drive to Chicago. Gas cost 72% of the total.

   a. Did she spend more than $150 on gasoline?

   _____

   Explain how you decided.

   _____

   _____

   b. Did she spend more than $200 on gasoline?

   _____

   _____

● Estimating Percents

For problems 1–5, choose the best answer for each problem. In the answer section at the bottom of the page, fill in the box of your choice.

1. Brian scored 79% on his last test. About how many of the 120 items on the test did he answer correctly?

   A 65   C 95
   B 80   D 105

2. Yolanda had $68 saved. She spent 44% of her savings on a gift for her mother. About how much did she spend for her mother's gift?

   J $20   L $40
   K $30   M $50

3. Anton is saving for a $480 bicycle. So far, he has saved 19% of the amount he needs. About how many dollars has he saved?

   A $91   C $136
   B $125   D $238

4. Of the 416 vehicles sold at Honest Hanna's last month, 28% were pick-up trucks. About how many pick-up trucks were sold last month?

   J 98   L 130
   K 116   M 202

5. Shiro says that 53% of the stamps in his collection are from the United States. If he has 2,600 stamps, about how many are from the United States?

   A 650   C 1,378
   B 1,222   D 1,550

Write About It

Explain how you would estimate the solution to this problem. Then solve.

6. In one week, 560 baskets of strawberries were picked at Strawberry Fields, and 73% of them were picked on the weekend. About how many baskets of strawberries were picked on the weekend?

   _____

   _____

   _____

   _____

   _____

© 1999 Metropolitan Teaching & Learning Co.

1. A☐ B☐ C☐ D☐   4. J☐ K☐ L☐ M☐
2. J☐ K☐ L☐ M☐   5. A☐ B☐ C☐ D☐
3. A☐ B☐ C☐ D☐

● Estimating Percents

Writing a Word Equation

You can write a word equation to help you solve percent problems.

Example

Wayne budgets 5% of his earnings to buy clothes.
If he earned $720 this week, how many dollars does
Wayne budget for clothes?

A. Write a word equation that tells the whole amount, the part, and the percent.

Whole x Percent = Part

B. Rewrite the word equation with amounts from the problem.

Whole	x	**Percent**	=	**Part**
↓		↓		↓
Amount Wayne earns	x	5%	=	Amount for clothes

C. Replace the words with numbers.

Whole	x	**Percent**	=	**Part**
Amount Wayne earns	x	5%	=	Amount for clothes
↓		↓		↓
$ _____	x	0.05	=	n

D. Solve the equation, and answer the question.

720 x 0.05 = _____

So, Wayne budgets $ _____ for clothes.

1. Michelle ordered 300 bricks for a wall. So far, 225 bricks have been delivered. What percent of the bricks have been delivered?

   a. Write the word equation with amounts from the problem.

Whole	x	Percent	=	Part
↓		↓		↓
Bricks needed	x	n	=	Bricks delivered

   b. Replace the words with numbers.

Bricks needed	x	n	=	Bricks delivered
↓		↓		↓
_____	x	n	=	_____

   c. Solve the equation. $300 \times n = 225$

   Divide both sides by 300. $\dfrac{300}{300} \times n = \dfrac{225}{300}$ So, $n = 0.75$, or 75%.

   So, 75% of the bricks have been delivered.

2. Luke needs 70 bricks to make a planter. He has 20% of the bricks he needs. How many bricks does he have?

   a. Write the word equation with amounts from the problem.

Whole	x	Percent	=	Part
↓		↓		↓
Bricks needed	x	20%	=	Bricks Luke has

   b. Replace the words with numbers.

Bricks needed	x	20%	=	Bricks Luke has
↓		↓		↓
_____	x	0.20	=	n

   c. Solve the equation. $70 \times 0.20 = $ _____

   So, Luke has _____ bricks.

PRACTICE

Write an equation to solve each problem.

3. Tina saves 15% of her earnings. She earned $640 last week. How many dollars will she put into savings?

_____

_____

4. Janice bought a video originally priced at $16 for 30% off. How much was the discount?

_____

_____

5. A camera is regularly priced at $148. It is on sale for 25% off. By how much is the price reduced?

_____

_____

6. Doreen counted 36 cows in a field. Of the cows, 27 were standing. What percent of the cows were standing?

_____

_____

7. There are 70 members of the Rose Society. At the last meeting, 28 members attended. What percent of the members attended?

_____

_____

8. Leon took out a loan of $2,000. He paid the bank 10% interest on the amount he borrowed. How much interest did he pay?

_____

_____

9. Of the $2,870 collected in a fund-raiser, 70% will pay for blankets for a homeless shelter. How many dollars will pay for blankets?

_____

_____

10. Francine bought a new car for 95% of the sticker price. She paid $15,200 for the car. What was the sticker price?

_____

_____

● Meaning of Percent

For problems 1–6, choose the best answer for each problem. In the answer section at the bottom of the page, fill in the box of your choice.

1. **Sales tax is 6%. Which equation could you use to find the sales tax on a $16 book?**

   A $16 ÷ 0.06 = sales tax
   B sales tax = $16 + 0.06
   C $16 x 0.06 = sales tax
   D sales tax = $16 x 6

2. **Julie has 72 videos. Of them, 18 are dramas. What percent of Julie's videos are dramas?**

   J 18%   L 45%
   K 25%   M 72%

3. **Francis is saving for a $120 keyboard. She has saved 35% of the money she needs. How much money has she saved?**

   A $35   C $55
   B $42   D $76

4. **A television is regularly priced at $450. It is on sale for 20% off. By how much is the price of the television reduced?**

   J $360   L $180
   K $240   M $90

5. **Mr. Platt bought 144 calendars for his store. He has sold 108 of them. What percent of the calendars have been sold?**

   A 108%   C 75%
   B 94%   D 36%

6. **Sales tax is 7%. How much is the sales tax on a dining room table that is priced at $300?**

   J $21   L $210
   K $37   M $307

Write About It

Explain how you could solve this problem, and then solve it.

7. **A carton holds 25 boxes of cereal. In one carton, 19 of the boxes are damaged. What percent of the boxes are damaged?**

   _____

   _____

   _____

   _____

   _____

1. A ☐ B ☐ C ☐ D ☐   4. J ☐ K ☐ L ☐ M ☐

2. J ☐ K ☐ L ☐ M ☐   5. A ☐ B ☐ C ☐ D ☐

3. A ☐ B ☐ C ☐ D ☐   6. J ☐ K ☐ L ☐ M ☐

● Meaning of Percent

Writing Word Equations

To solve problems with more than two steps, you can decide what to do first by making a list of the questions you need to answer.

In this example, you will need to use information from the advertisement at the right.

Example

Sarah gave the cashier $200 dollars for a CD changer that was on sale. How much change did she receive?

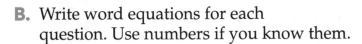

A. Make a list of the questions you need to answer.

- **How much change did she receive?**

- **How much did she pay?**

- **How much is 20% off?**

B. Write word equations for each question. Use numbers if you know them.

Change	=	$200	–	**Cost**
Paid	=	$220	–	**(20% off)**
20% off	=	0.20	x	$220

C. Decide which question is easiest to answer first.

THINK: **I know the numbers to calculate 20% off.**

0.20 x $220 = $ _____

D. Use what you calculated to answer the other questions and solve the problem.

Paid	=	$220	–	$ _____	=	$ _____
Change	=	$200	–	$ _____	=	$ _____

So, Sarah received $ _____ in change.

GUIDED PRACTICE

The graph shows percentages of 200 votes. Greg carved entries C and D.

1. How many votes did Greg's pumpkins get?

   a. Underline the questions you need to answer.

   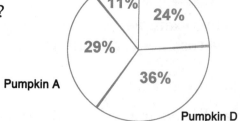

   - How many votes did Greg's Pumpkins get?

   - How many votes did pumpkin A get?

   - How many votes did pumpkin C get?

   - How many votes did pumpkin D get?

   b. Write word equations for each amount that you need to find.

   Votes for Greg's pumpkins = _____ + _____

   Votes for pumpkin C = _____ x 200

   Votes for pumpkin D = _____ x 200

   c. Decide what to do first. Calculate votes for _____.

   d. Solve the equations, and answer the question.

   How many votes did Greg's pumpkins get? _____

2. How many more votes did Greg's pumpkin D get than pumpkin A?

   a. Write the questions you need to answer.

   _____

   _____

   b. Write word equations for each amount that you need to find.

   _____

   _____

   c. Decide what to do first. Then finish solving the problem.

   _____

   _____

   So, Greg's pumpkin D won by _____ votes.

PRACTICE

As you solve these problems, use what you know to decide which question to answer first.

3. If sales tax is 6%, what is the total cost of a CD player that costs $120 and a CD that costs $15?

   a. Underline the question that you will answer first.

   ● How much are the two items without tax?

   ● How much are the two items with tax?

   b. Solve the problem.

   _____

   _____

   So, the total cost for the 2 items is $ _____ .

Solve . . . .

4. Tony got 70% of the 20 problems right on his first math test. He got 19 out of 20 right on the second test. **How many more problems did he get right on the second test?**

   _____

5. Marcia bought 2 CDs for $16.00 each and a tape for $8.00. The sales tax is 6%. **What was the total cost?**

   _____

Use the circle graph for problems 6–8. The graph shows percentages of 250 votes.

6. In an election, 250 club members voted. **By how many votes did Marquis win the election?**

   _____

7. **In total, how many votes did Forrester and Cox get?**

   _____

8. **How many more votes did Forrester get than Cox?**

   _____

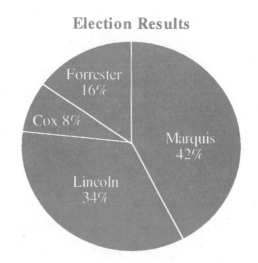

Election Results

Forrester 16%

Cox 8%

Marquis 42%

Lincoln 34%

● Finding the Percent of a Number

For problems 1–5, choose the best answer for each problem. In the answer section at the bottom of the page, fill in the box of your choice.

1. Scott bought a shirt for $24. Sales tax was 6%. What was the total cost of the shirt?

   A $1.44   C $25.44
   B $22.56   D $38.40

2. Nadia bought a fan for $30 and a radio for $90. The sales tax was 5%. What was the total cost?

   J $109   L $148
   K $126   M $180

3. A model airplane regularly priced at $15.90 is on sale for 40% off. What is the sale price?

   A $6.36   C $8.75
   B $7.95   D $9.54

4. At a 50%-off sale, Jackie bought items originally priced at $16 and $8.40. How much did Jackie spend?

   J $7.60   L $16.40
   K $12.20   M $24.40

5. Of Audrey's note cards, 30% have animals on them, and 25% of the note cards have flowers on them. Audrey has 40 note cards. How many have either animals or flowers on them?

   A 2   C 20
   B 18   D 22

Write About It

Explain how you would decide what to do first to solve this problem.

6. Robert had 80 baseball cards. He gave 25% of them to his sister. Then he bought 10 more. How many cards does Robert have now?

   _____

   _____

   _____

1. A ☐ B ☐ C ☐ D ☐   4. J ☐ K ☐ L ☐ M ☐

2. J ☐ K ☐ L ☐ M ☐   5. A ☐ B ☐ C ☐ D ☐

3. A ☐ B ☐ C ☐ D ☐

● Finding the Percent of a Number

Test-Taking Skill: Writing a Plan

On some tests, you need to explain how to solve a problem. It is important to explain your thinking and show your calculations.

Example

Keesha made trail mix. She began with $2\frac{1}{2}$ cups of oatmeal and added 2 cups of nuts, $1\frac{1}{2}$ cups of raisins, $2\frac{1}{4}$ cups of chocolate bits, $1\frac{3}{4}$ cups of sunflower seeds. She put the mix into 4 bags of equal size. How much mix did Keesha put into each bag?

A. Read the problem carefully. Decide on the kind of answer you need.

The answer is the amount of trail mix in each bag.

B. Write a plan for finding the answer.

First, I will add all the ingredients to find the total amount of mix.

Then, I will divide the total by 4 to find how many cups of trail mix Keesha put into each bag.

C. Solve the problem. Show your thinking and your calculations. Change your plan if you need to.

1: $2\frac{1}{2} + 2 + 1\frac{1}{2} + 2\frac{1}{4} + 1\frac{3}{4} = 10$

2: $10 \div 4 =$ _____

D. Remember to answer the question in the problem.

Keesha put _____ cups of mix into each bag.

TEST-TAKING PRACTICE

Write a plan to solve each problem. Explain your thinking.
Then solve.

1. Tara added $3\frac{1}{3}$ cups of flour and 2 cups of milk to the mixing bowl. Now, there are $7\frac{2}{3}$ cups of batter in the bowl. **How much batter was in the bowl before she added the flour?**

   _____

   _____

   _____

   _____

   _____

   _____

   _____

   _____

   _____

   _____

2. Sid weighed his puppy each week. At first, the puppy weighed $3\frac{1}{4}$ pounds. It gained $\frac{3}{4}$ of a pound every week for 3 weeks. The fourth week, it gained $1\frac{1}{4}$ pounds. **How much did the puppy weigh after four weeks?**

   _____

   _____

   _____

   _____

   _____

   _____

3. Leda has 5 scallop shells, 4 fan shells, and 7 oyster shells. **What fraction of her collection is fan shells?**

   _____

   _____

   _____

   _____

   _____

   _____

© 1999 Metropolitan Teaching & Learning Co.

● Test-Taking Skill

Using Formulas

Sometimes, you must use a formula to solve a problem. Shown below are some formulas for finding perimeter (*P*) and area (*A*). The variables in a formula are often chosen so that the meaning of each letter is easy to remember. In these formulas, *l* stands for length, *w* stands for width, and *h* stands for height.

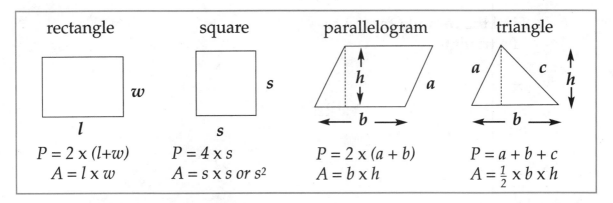

rectangle	square	parallelogram	triangle
$P = 2 \times (l+w)$	$P = 4 \times s$	$P = 2 \times (a + b)$	$P = a + b + c$
$A = l \times w$	$A = s \times s$ or s^2	$A = b \times h$	$A = \frac{1}{2} \times b \times h$

Example 1

Mr. Winston has a rectangular garden 20 ft long and 12 ft wide. How many feet of fencing will he need to completely surround the garden?

A. Decide which formula to use for the perimeter of a rectangle.

THINK: The length of the border of a figure is the perimeter.

$P =$ _____

B. Substitute the values for *l* and *w* that are given in the problem, and solve.

$P = 2 \times ($ _____ + _____)   so, $P = 2 \times (32) = 64$

So, he will need _____ ft of fencing.

Example 2

Each side of a square playground measures 20 m. What is the perimeter of the playground?

Step 1: Find the formula for the perimeter of a square. $P =$ _____

Step 2: Substitute values for *s*, and solve. $P = 4 \times$ _____ So, $P = 80$

So, the perimeter of the playground is _____ m.

Use the table of formulas on the next page to solve these problems.

1. A triangular sail has a height of 14 ft and a base
    of 8 ft. What is the area of the sail?

   Step 1: **Find the formula for the area
   of a triangle.**

   $A =$ _____

   Step 2: **Substitute the known values for
   b and h, and solve.**

   $A = \frac{1}{2}$ x _____ x _____

   So, $A = 4 \times 14 =$ _____.

   So, the sail has an area of _____ sq ft.

> Notice that area is measured in
> square units. Some units of area
> include square centimeters (cm^2),
> square inches (in.^{2}), and
> square feet (ft^2).

2. A square photograph has sides measuring 8 in.
    How many square inches of glass would you
    need in a frame for the photo?

   Step 1: **Find the formula for the area of a square.**

   $A = s^2$ or _____

   Step 2: **Substitute the known values for s, and solve.**

   $A =$ _____ x _____   So, $A = 64$.

   So, you would need _____ square inches of glass.

PRACTICE

Use a formula from the table to solve each problem. Write down the formula you used and the solution.

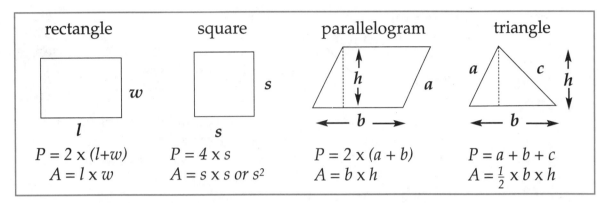

rectangle	square	parallelogram	triangle
$P = 2 \times (l+w)$	$P = 4 \times s$	$P = 2 \times (a + b)$	$P = a + b + c$
$A = l \times w$	$A = s \times s \ or \ s^2$	$A = b \times h$	$A = \frac{1}{2} \times b \times h$

3. A triangular flag has a base of 4 ft and a height of 9 ft. What is the area of the flag?

   _____

   _____

4. The sides of a square field measure 60 m. How many meters of fence are needed for the field?

   _____

   _____

5. A rectangular quilt measures 1.5 m by 2 m. How many meters of ribbon would be needed to sew around the border of the quilt?

   _____

   _____

6. A parallelogram has a height of 12 cm and a base of 20 cm. What is the area of the parallelogram?

   _____

   _____

7. The sides of a triangular traffic island are 30 ft, 40, ft, and 42 ft. What is its perimeter?

   _____

   _____

8. A rectangular wall is 9 ft high and 14 feet long. What is the area of the wall?

   _____

   _____

Choose the best solution for each problem. Fill in the box of your choice in the answer section at the bottom of this page. You can find the formulas in the table on the previous page.

1. A rectangular parking lot measures 40 yd by 30 yd. What is its perimeter?

    A 70 yd   C 210 yd

    B 140 yd   D 1,200 yd

2. Will wants to know the area of his square garden so that he can decide how much fertilizer to use. The sides of the garden measure 15 ft. What is its area?

    J 30 ft   L 225 ft

    K 60 ft   M 225 sq ft

3. The floor in a room measures 4 yd by 3 yd. Carpeting is sold by the square yard. How much carpeting will cover the floor?

    A 6 sq yd   C 14 sq yd

    B 12 sq yd   D 24 sq yd

4. The sides of a triangular shawl measure 40 in., 65 in., and 40 in. How many inches of trim are needed for the border?

    J 40 in.   L 145 in.

    K 105 in.   M 800 sq in.

Write About It

Write a plan for solving the following problem. Then solve.

5. A triangular road sign has a base measuring 15 in. Its height is 12 in. What is the area of the road sign?

    _____

    _____

    _____

    _____

    _____

    _____

1. A ☐   B ☐   C ☐   D ☐   3. A ☐   B ☐   C ☐   D ☐

2. J ☐   K ☐   L ☐   M ☐   4. J ☐   K ☐   L ☐   M ☐

● Multiplication

Drawing Examples

Some problems will ask you to decide whether a statement about a geometrical figure is true or not. Drawing examples of the figure can help you reach the correct answer.

Example

Is this statement true or false?

A quadrilateral always has two diagonals.

A. Try to draw a figure to support the statement.
A quadrilateral has 4 sides.
Draw a regular quadrilateral—a square.

THINK: A diagonal connects opposite vertices.
Draw diagonals in the square.
How many diagonals did you draw? _____

B. Try to draw a figure that does not support the statement.

Draw some more quadrilaterals, and construct their diagonals.
Try to draw a quadrilateral that does not have two diagonals.

C. Refer to the figures you drew.

Could you draw a quadrilateral that doesn't have 2 diagonals?

_____

Is the statement true or false? _____

1. Is the following statement *sometimes true, always true,* or *never true*?

   <u>Intersecting lines are perpendicular.</u>

   Step 1: Try to draw a figure that supports the statement.
   Draw two intersecting lines that are perpendicular.
   THINK: Lines that are perpendicular form a right angle.

   Can you draw intersecting lines that are perpendicular? _____

   Step 2: Try to draw a figure that doesn't support the statement.
   Draw two intersecting lines that are <u>not</u> perpendicular.

   Can you draw intersecting lines that are not perpendicular? _____

   Step 3: Refer to the figures you drew.
   Is the statement *sometimes true, always true,* or *never true*?

   _____

2. Is the following statement *sometimes true, always true,* or
   never true? <u>A triangle has 2 right angles</u>.

   Step 1: Try to draw a figure that supports the statement.
   Draw the base of a triangle. Draw a right angle at each end.

   Can you draw a triangle with 2 right angles? _____

   Step 2: Refer to the figures you drew.

   Is the statement *sometimes true, always true,* or *never true*?

   _____

PRACTICE

Draw examples to help you decide whether each statement is *true* or *false*.

Decide whether each statement is *sometimes true, always true,* or *never true.*

3. **A quadrilateral with 3 right angles is a rectangle.**

7. **A quadrilateral with four congruent sides is a square.**

_____

_____

4. **Two of the sides of a triangle can be parallel.**

8. **A triangle with an obtuse angle is a right triangle.**

_____

_____

5. **A triangle has one diagonal.**

9. **A square has four right angles.**

_____

_____

6. **A right triangle can have three congruent sides.**

10. **An isosceles triangle has two right angles.**

_____

_____

TEST-TAKING PRACTICE

Choose the best solution for each problem. In the answer section at the bottom of this page, fill in the box of your choice.

1. **If a quadrilateral has four congruent sides, it has four congruent angles.**

   A Always True
   B Sometimes True
   C Never True

2. **A quadrilateral with four unequal sides is a parallelogram.**

   J Always True
   K Sometimes True
   L Never True

3. **A quadrilateral with two right angles is a rectangle.**

   A Always True
   B Sometimes True
   C Never True

4. **If a triangle has three congruent angles, it has three congruent sides.**

   J Always True
   K Sometimes True
   L Never True

5. **A quadrilateral with four right angles is a parallelogram.**

   A Always True
   B Sometimes True
   C Never True

6. **A right triangle is an isosceles triangle.**

   J Always True
   K Sometimes True
   L Never True

Write About It

Explain how you could draw examples to decide whether the following statement is true or false.

7. **A triangle with no congruent sides cannot be a right triangle.**

_____

_____

_____

_____

_____

_____

_____

© 1999 Metropolitan Teaching & Learning Co.

1. A ☐ B ☐ C ☐
2. J ☐ K ☐ L ☐
3. A ☐ B ☐ C ☐
4. J ☐ K ☐ L ☐
5. A ☐ B ☐ C ☐
6. J ☐ K ☐ L ☐

● Quadrilaterals

Making a Table to Show Possible Outcomes

For some problems, you need to find all the ways that two events could turn out. You can show the possible outcomes for two events in a table.

Example

This table shows the possible outcomes for spinning the two spinners.

Spinner 2

	1	2	3	4	5
A	(A, 1)	(A, 2)	(A, 3)	(A, 4)	(A, 5)
B	(B, 1)	(B, 2)	(B, 3)	(B, 4)	(B, 5)
C	(C, 1)	(C, 2)	(C, 3)	(C, 4)	(C, 5)
D	(D, 1)	(D, 2)	(D, 3)	(D, 4)	(D, 5)
E	(E, 1)	(E, 2)	(E, 3)	(E, 4)	(E, 5)
F	(F, 1)	(F, 2)	(F, 3)	(F, 4)	(F, 5)

Spinner 1

A. The outcomes for the numbered spinner are column labels in the table.

What are the column labels? _____

The outcomes for the lettered spinner are row labels in the table.

What are the row labels? _____

B. At the intersection of each row and column is a letter-number pair called an ordered pair that shows a result of spinning the two spinners. Each ordered pair is written the same way.

What is the ordered pair for the result displayed on the spinners? _____

C. **How are the outcomes the same in row D?** _____

How are they different? _____

How are the outcomes the same in column 3? _____

How are they different? _____

D. The table shows all of the outcomes possible if you spin the two spinners.

How many outcomes are there in the table? _____

So, there are _____ **possible outcomes.**

• Listing Outcomes

GUIDED PRACTICE

Bonnie has red, black, blue, green, yellow, and brown collars for her dog. She has red, black, and blue leashes. Make a table to show the possible collar-and-leash choices that Bonnie can make.

1. **Label the rows with the collar colors.**

   Label the columns with the leash colors.

2. **Complete the table. Write the collar-leash outcomes.**

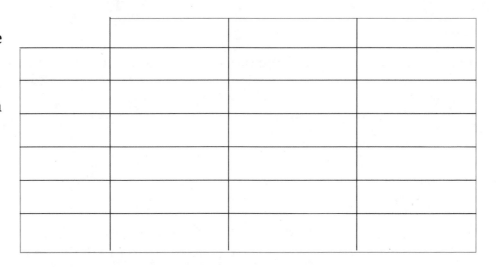

3. **How many collar-leash outcomes are possible?** _____

4. **In how many outcomes are the collar and leash the same color?** _____

5. **Can Bonnie use a green leash with a red collar?** _____

Make a table to show all the possible outcomes if you draw one item from each of these bags.

APPLE PEACH PEAR   CIRCLE SQUARE STAR

6. **Label the rows and columns.**

7. **Complete the table to show the outcomes for drawing one item from each bag.**

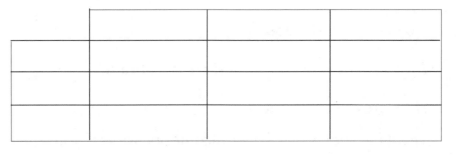

8. **How many possible outcomes are there?** _____

PRACTICE

Make a table to show the possible outcomes for each pair of events.

9. **Suppose you spin the STAR and NUMBER spinners. In how many of the possible outcomes are both letters vowels (*a, e, i, o,* or *u*)?**

_____

10. **In how many outcomes is at least one letter a vowel?** _____

11. **Suppose a name is drawn from each hat below. In how many of the possible outcomes is one name a boy and the other a girl? (In this case, Alex is a boy.)** _____

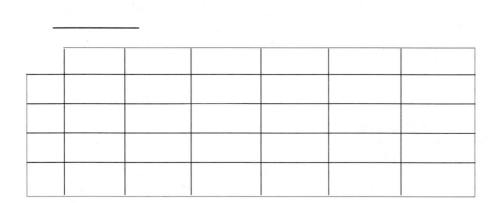

12. **In how many outcomes are both of the names girls' names?** _____

13. **In how many outcomes is at least one name a boy's name?** _____

Choose the best answer for each problem. In the answer section at the bottom of this page, fill in the box of your choice.

For problems 1–4, suppose you take a card from each group.

1. **How many outcomes are possible?**

   A 5   C 25
   B 10   D 50

2. **In how many outcomes do both cards show animals?**

   J 2   L 6
   K 4   M 8

3. **In how many outcomes is at least one of the cards a flower?**

   A 1   C 9
   B 5   D 10

4. **In how many outcomes is one card an animal and the other a flower?**

   J 2   L 6
   K 4   M 8

5. **If you have three colors of shoes and 4 colors of socks, how many possible shoe-sock outcomes are there?**

   A 6   C 12
   B 7   D 24

Write About It

6. **Suppose you can choose from red, yellow, or green socks. You can also choose boots, sneakers, sandals, or slippers. Explain how you would set up a table to find all of the possible sock-shoe outcomes.**

   _____

   _____

   _____

   _____

   _____

   _____

1. A ☐   B ☐   C ☐   D ☐   4. J ☐   K ☐   L ☐   M ☐

2. J ☐   K ☐   L ☐   M ☐   5. A ☐   B ☐   C ☐   D ☐

3. A ☐   B ☐   C ☐   D ☐

Name _____

Making a Tree Diagram

Sometimes you need to find all the ways that three or more events could turn out. For these problems, a tree diagram is more helpful than a table for seeing all the possibilities.

Example

Suppose you flip a dime, a nickel, and a penny. In how many of the possible outcomes does at least one coin show tails?

A. The first event is flipping a dime.

The possible outcomes are heads and tails.

Write the event and the possible outcomes.

Dime
H
T

B. The second event is flipping a nickel.

For both dime outcomes, draw a branch to show heads and tails for the nickel.

What are the possible outcomes if you flip a dime and a nickel?

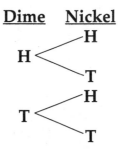

(H, H); (H, T); _____ ; _____

C. Continue the tree diagram to show the possible outcomes for flipping a penny. Then write the outcomes for all three coins.

Complete the list of outcomes.

D. How many possible outcomes are there for flipping 3 coins?

_____

E. In how many outcomes is there at least one tails result?

_____

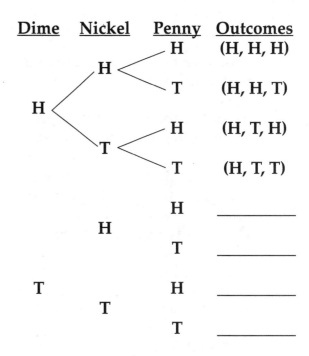

© 1999 Metropolitan Teaching & Learning Co.

GUIDED PRACTICE

Suppose you spin each of these spinners. In how many of the possible outcomes do exactly two spinners show red?

1. **What are the possible outcomes for spinner A? Complete the list of them in the tree diagram.**

Spinner A	Spinner B	Spinner C	Possible Outcomes
		Red	(Red, Red, Red)
	Red	Yellow	(Red, Red, Yellow)
Red		Red	(Red, Blue, Red)
	Blue	Yellow	(Red, Blue, Yellow)

2. **What are the possible outcomes for spinner B? Complete the branches to match the outcomes for spinner A with each of the outcomes for spinner B.**

3. **What are the possible outcomes for spinner C? Complete the branches to include the outcomes for Spinner C.**

4. **Follow each branch of the tree diagram. Complete the list of possible outcomes for spinning the three spinners.**

5. **How many possible outcomes are there for spinning the three spinners?**

   _____

6. **In how many of the possible outcomes do exactly two of the spinners**

   show red? _____

PRACTICE

Suppose you draw a ball from each bag.

7. **Make a tree diagram to show all of the possible outcomes.**

Bag A	Bag B	Bag C	Possible Outcomes
		1	

Use your tree diagram to answer these questions.

8. **How many outcomes are possible?** _____

9. **In how many outcomes are all three numbers the same?** _____

10. **In how many outcomes are there at least two 2s?** _____

• Listing Outcomes

Choose the best answer for each problem. In the answer section
at the bottom of this page, fill in the box of your choice.

Use this experiment for problems
1–5. Suppose you drew a letter from
each box.

| E A R | O R | O R E |

1. **How many outcomes are
    possible?**
    A 8   C 12
    B 9   D 18

2. **For how many outcomes will all
    of the letters drawn be the same?**
    J 1   L 4
    K 2   M 5

3. **For how many outcomes are at
    least two of the letters *R*s?**
    A 4   C 6
    B 5   D 7

4. **In how many outcomes is at least
    one letter an *O*?**
    J 6   L 9
    K 8   M 12

5. **In how many outcomes is one
    letter an *A*?**
    A 6   C 9
    B 8   D 12

Write About It

Explain how you would make a tree
diagram to solve this problem.

6. **Suppose you toss three counters
    that are red on one side and blue
    on the other side. In how many
    possible outcomes will at least
    one counter show red?**

_____

_____

_____

_____

_____

_____

_____

_____

1. A ☐ B ☐ C ☐ D ☐   4. J ☐ K ☐ L ☐ M ☐

2. J ☐ K ☐ L ☐ M ☐   5. A ☐ B ☐ C ☐ D ☐

3. A ☐ B ☐ C ☐ D ☐

● Listing Outcomes

Test-Taking Skill: Trying Out the Answer Choices

If you have trouble solving a problem or finding an answer, decide on the kind of answer you need. Then, try out the different answer choices. This method can help you find the correct answer.

Example

The stadium seats 74,000. For the game, about 52,000 tickets were sold. About what percent of the stadium's capacity was that?

A 22,000 seats **C** 70%
B 30% **D** 100%

Step 1: **Decide on the kind of answer you need.**

The answer will be a percent.

Step 2: **Try each answer choice.**

Choice	Think	Is this the answer?
A: 22,000 seats	This is the wrong kind of answer.	No, the question asks for a percent.
B: 30%	An estimate, $\frac{1}{3}$ of 75,000 = 25,000, gives too small a number.	No, 30% of 74,000 is about 25,000.
C: 70%	Multiply: 0.7 x 74,000 = _____	Yes, 70% of 74,000 is 51,800. That's about right.
D: 100%	This cannot be the answer.	No, not all the seats were filled.

Step 3: Choose the correct answer, and fill in the correct square in the answer section.

1. A☐ B☐ C☐ D☐

TEST-TAKING PRACTICE

Choose the best answer for each problem. In the answer section
at the bottom of this page, fill in the box of your choice.

1. Marta wants to leave a 20% tip at
a restaurant. The bill is for $7.95.
How much should she leave?

   A $0.80   C $3.20
   B $1.60   D $7.95

2. In 1997, 70% of the music albums
sold were CDs. Just 4 years
earlier, CDs had 20% less of the
market. **What percent of albums
sold in 1993 were CDs?**

   J 20%   L 60%
   K 50%   M 70%

3. Pele made the exact color of red
he wanted by mixing 6 drops of
Scarlet paint with 4 drops of Fire
Orange. He has 12 jars of Scarlet.
**How many jars of Fire Orange
does he need to mix with the
Scarlet to make the same
shade?**

   A 4 jars   C 8 jars
   B 6 jars   D 12 jars

4. Bernie spent 2 hours doing his
homework. He spent $\frac{1}{3}$ of that
time on his math homework.
How long did it take him to do
his math homework?

   J 6 minutes   L 20 minutes
   K 12 minutes   M 40 minutes

5. Nancy has a recipe that calls for
2 cups of nuts for every 6 cups of
dough. She wants to use 8 cups of
nuts. **How much dough does she
need?**

   A 8 cups   C 24 cups
   B 12 cups   D 48 cups

6. Ralph needs new socks.
Sockorama sells 3 pairs for $7.50.
The Sox Box has a sale on
4 pairs for 20% off its regular
price of $10.00. **Where will Ralph
get the best buy on one dozen
pairs of socks?**

   J Sockorama   L $24.00
   K The Sox Box   M $30.00

1. A☐ B☐ C☐ D☐   4. J☐ K☐ L☐ M☐
2. J☐ K☐ L☐ M☐   5. A☐ B☐ C☐ D☐
3. A☐ B☐ C☐ D☐   6. J☐ K☐ L☐ M☐

© 1999 Metropolitan Teaching & Learning Co.

• Test-Taking Skill